My Life at Kings Point

The Longest Days and The Shortest Years

By
Gustave Jockers
USMMA
Class of 1971

ACKNOWLEDGEMENTS

I'd like to thank Midships 1971 for a few of the photos that I used in this book to show some of the activities that took place during our four-year experience at Kings Point. I want to also thank several of my friends for carefully reading and providing constructive feedback to help me keep moving forward. They include John, Sully, Duck, Ben, and my biggest supporter Tommy.

The background information about the taking of USS Pueblo by North Korea at the beginning of Chapter 3 Third Class Sea Year, was mainly posted on the usspueblo.org website. This is noted by asterisks following the section recounting the events leading up to the capture and imprisonment of the crew and officers of USS Pueblo for 335 days. I strongly encourage readers to learn more about this historic event.

PREFACE

I did not set out to write a book about my four years at Kings Point. It started as a single short chapter about my early years before starting my career. I was preparing to write about my experiences in manufacturing in American companies and those in other parts of the world with a focus on Asia. I was urged by my college roommate, my close friend, and confidant, Tom McCabe, to focus my attention on the US Merchant Marine Academy four-year period and tell some stories about those experiences.

After researching the books written about Kings Point, I was shocked to discover that almost nothing had been written and none by a graduate with all of the gruesome details. I've read a number of books about the other service academies both fiction and nonfiction. You'll discover, Kings Point is an unusual military college to attend, and all alumni treasure the experience for a variety of reasons.

As a baby boomer and an engineer, I've tried to remain as current as I could throughout my career with the dramatic changes in technology. Generation X will remember things like a telephone in the kitchen with a cord on it and pay bills by snail mail and a postage stamp. For most millennials, their perspective differs dramatically, and they have to rely on what they read, view on YouTube or hear stories from their parents and relatives. Today's expedient means of communication and social interaction is a total change from the previous two generations.

I came of age in the 1960s, so demonstrations and even riots do not disturb or traumatize me. I lived through the assassination of some of the most influential people of our time, I grew up in the exact location where the Woodstock event of 1969 took place, and I saw our brightest people work with national purpose to land men on the moon and bring them back to Earth safely. As a youngster, our telephone had no dial or buttons, and we told a live operator the 4-digit number we wanted to call. I currently use an iPhone, iPad, Mac desktop and the latest digital still life/video camera and I know how to make them share information as though I grew up using them. I first started my passion for photography when I was very young and evolved into video when it became instant playback. I've always kept my pictures and videos organized and used many of them in this novella to illustrate a point or to help bring stories to life.

I graduated from Kings Point in 1971. It was the last engineering class in our history to graduate using only a slide rule. Portable calculators were not available until September of the year I graduated – a few months too late! I traveled extensively throughout my career and still do. I will continue my efforts to complete the book I started to write until I got sidetracked preparing My Life at Kings Point. I plan to explain why there are hundreds of thousands of manufacturing jobs that departed in the final two decades of the previous century that will never return to America, the part I played, and why I know, they will not be coming back.

Chapter 1
My Early Years
Growing Up

I grew up in the Hudson River Valley of upstate New York in the small village of Orange Lake with my parents and three sisters. I was child number three and a baby boomer born in 1949. Like many people my age, my dad was a combat veteran of WWII. He was raised in the same town where I grew up, but unlike our parents, his parents didn't have the incentive and motivation to help him achieve all that he could. When he was growing up, he wanted to attend the U.S. Military Academy at West Point located only about 20 miles away. Times were very different in the 1930s, and he just didn't know how to maneuver his way by himself through the complicated process of getting a congressional nomination to attend West Point.

Instead, after graduation from high school, he joined the US Army and approached his goal and passion in life from a different direction. From a very young age, his strong desire was to be an airplane pilot, and he received his flight training in the Army Air Corps. The U.S. Air Force branch of the military didn't exist until 1949. My dad was an excellent pilot and also an excellent communicator and patient teacher. Eventually, he was chosen by the Army to be a flight instructor, which was a significant position in the United States Army Air Corps leading up December 7, 1941, when America declared war on Japan.

During the WWII, my father "Flew the Hump" which we heard many times growing up, but I was well into my adulthood before I could understand the importance of his activities and achievements. The "Hump" was the nickname for the Himalayan Mountains that Allied pilots flew over with military transport aircraft from India to China. The joint Allied effort was to resupply the Allied Air Forces lead by the US Army Air Corps and the Chinese war effort led by Chiang Kai-shek in the China Theater against the Japanese. Just imagine the danger of flying over those mountains with very limited navigational aids and charts. Weather reporting and radio communication were unreliable and extremely spotty. Until I learned in my mid-30s the importance of the work my dad and others accomplished in this strategic war effort, he had already passed away. One of my life regrets is that I couldn't share with my father the things I had finally learned and genuinely grasped about his experiences during World War II. I eventually learned how badly the Japanese decimated the Chinese before and during WWII by reading and researching this history. In school, our history classes focused much more on European history, and little effort placed on Asia and the Middle East. Immediately following the surrender of Japan on September 2, 1945, the Chinese Civil War resumed. The Civil War pitted the communist Mao Zedong and his Red Chinese army against Chiang Kai-shek and his freedom seeking followers.

My father's very first pilot assignment for the Army was in Memphis, Tennessee where the US Army Air Corps was using the civilian runways to land and ferry newly-built aircraft from the mid-west factories to rail yards in preparation for shipment overseas. Today, that airport is the Memphis International Airport and the hub of Federal Express. Before my dad got reassigned to Memphis, he and my mother (high school sweethearts) were married. My mom was all of 18 and Dad was 22. In August 1942, while stationed in Memphis, my oldest sister was born, and my mom returned to upstate New York to live briefly with my paternal Grandparents which was a painful period in my mother's life. She did not know her in-laws very well, they were difficult people to live with, and they were unpleasant to my mother and my newborn sister. My mother couldn't wait to rejoin my father.

After receiving a promotion to become a full-time flight instructor, my father got transferred from Memphis to Homestead Air Base in Homestead, Florida outside of Miami. As soon as my father relocated to Homestead, my mother and their new baby joined my father in Southern Florida. He taught other pilots how to fly the workhorse Douglas C-54 Skymasters over the "Hump" from Burma to China. Eventually, he got assigned to the war zone where he flew "The Hump" himself. It was very common during the war for young wives and children to join their husbands during their station stateside. It was too expensive to rent an entire apartment, so many of the young servicemen rented a room for their spouse, and they were able to enjoy the privilege of using other common rooms of the local homeowner to fill the war year needs of temporary housing. My parents rented a room with house privileges from an older couple named Mr. and Mrs. Case, at their home located in Coral Gables close to the air base where my dad trained pilots. After my father transferred overseas, my mother and sister continued to stay in Southern Florida with the Cases. My mother was in her early twenties, and she grew very close to the Cases in the years my father was overseas. They were so close that my mother called Mrs. Case "Mom Case" and they remained close for the remainder of Mrs. Case's life.

I didn't understand this story as a youngster, but I vividly remember taking several long car trips with my parents and sisters from our home in upstate New York to Miami to spend time with Mrs. Case. Mr. Case passed away shortly after the war ended and she stayed in the same home that my mother lived in during my father's absence. In the 1950s, before the Interstate Highway system existed, the trip took three days by car each way. My sisters and I fondly remember those long trips and some of the things we learned along the way. We also grew to love Mrs. Case who was my mother's second Mom.

After the war finally ended and my father returned, my parents put everything they could beg and borrow to purchase Stateside Airways in Orange Lake, New York along with two airplanes – a Piper Cub and a Stinson. As far back as I can remember, I thought everybody had planes in their backyard. Along with my two older sisters, we were always busy,

7

especially in the summertime. Orange Lake was a vacation destination primarily for people who traveled 60 miles from New York City either by boat along the Hudson River or by train. Small airplanes were a big attraction for people to watch taking off and land and maybe take a ride themselves. We had two gas pumps in front of our little house and a small stand to sell hot dogs and ice cream, and it was always busy.

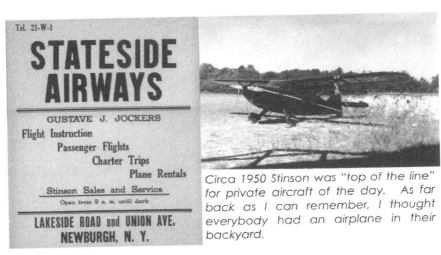

Tel. 21-W-1

STATESIDE AIRWAYS

GUSTAVE J. JOCKERS

Flight Instruction
Passenger Flights
Charter Trips
Plane Rentals

Stinson Sales and Service

Open from 9 a. m. until dark

LAKESIDE ROAD and UNION AVE.
NEWBURGH, N. Y.

Circa 1950 Stinson was "top of the line" for private aircraft of the day. As far back as I can remember, I thought everybody had an airplane in their backyard.

This exciting time as a child was short-lived and by the time I was 5 or 6 the airplanes were gone. It was fun for people to take a short ride, or watch the take-offs and landings while enjoying a hot dog and soda. However, those who would pay to learn to fly or rent an airplane were far too limited, and snack food couldn't support the mortgages my parents had taken out. Since I'm a Jr., my mom didn't want people calling me "Little Gus" or "Gussie." With the middle name John, my family and close friends always called me Jack or Jackie.

Sandi, P.A. and Jack circa 1952

Work Ethic

Work ethic isn't taught or imparted. Instead, it evolves. Learning how to perform a job that gives you satisfaction by either seeing the results physically or teaching others to accomplish a task with expertise is rewarding. After repeating the process over and over the end product continues to get better. Before you know it, you develop a love of the process and look forward to each new day.

Enjoyment of work is one of the most important things I learned from my parents as a youngster. I recall, no matter what the weather, we would be outside from sunup to sundown. It seemed there was always all kinds of activity and it wasn't thought of as work as much as participation. I learned to put gas in the small airplanes and then I wanted to do it all the time. I learned how to do something well, and both of my parents were good at giving thanks and a "job well done" to support the performance. My older sisters used to work in the hot dog stand in the summer. They sold hot dogs and ice cream to people watching the air-planes. I couldn't do that job because I couldn't reach the counter. Sadly, by the time I could reach the serving counter, the hot dog stand was sealed up, and the airplanes were gone. When we were tired and dirty at the end of the day, we often walked around together as a family and reviewed the fruits of our efforts and felt a strong sense of accomplishment. I have never been able to shake that habit.

After the runway was inactive, my Dad and I always kept the maintenance equipment in good running order. An assigned chore for me, as a kid, was to mow the runway. This cherished photo of my son, Ben, and I mowing Grandpa's runway. photo:1977

My father grew up less than five miles from our home, and his parents lived their entire lives and eventually died in the same house. He was one of two children and an only son. My mother was the oldest of nine children, and my oldest sister was older than two of her uncles! My mother's family lived less than half a mile from our home. As a result, I grew up with nine sets of aunts and uncles and a large number of great aunts and uncles. Before the 1970s, nearly everyone stayed in the area where they were born and raised. My next older sister was the first person in this enormous family to graduate from college in 1969.

My dad's father was a union carpenter and third generation immigrant. My mom's father was also a carpenter, but he was non-union and owned his own business. There was a distinct difference between my two grandfathers. My mom used to say that my Grandpa Jockers retired at 62 and then sat down in his comfortable chair, smoked his pipe and watched baseball for 32 years until he died. Meanwhile, my Grandpa Ahlers worked almost until he died in his mid-80s. I worked several summers while in high school for my grandfather and uncles in their carpenter business, Wm Ahlers & Sons. Each uncle had a building specialty, and I learned things I still use to this day. It's all about the genes!

While my dad was never a professional carpenter, he indeed was good at carpentry, and he was a perfectionist. He was also an excellent mechanic. It's similar to the situation of a family farmer who has to be a jack of all trades. My father fixed not just his airplanes, but all of the maintenance equipment that was needed to operate and maintain a grass strip airport in both the warm summer months and the cold and snowy upstate New York winters. By working hand-in-hand with my dad for many years putting extensions on our house, upgrading and maintaining cars, tractors and various equipment — I too became a perfectionist and a jack of all trades.

The house we lived in during the 1950s with four young kids measured 20' x 20' or 400 square feet. To make it to the attic bedroom, we had to use a pull-down stairway into the kitchen. To give perspective, the house that my wife and I had built for us in 1984; the family room is larger than 400 square feet! That's not unusual for today's standard size homes. From that simple small frame, in the late 1950s, we added a significant extension for a living room. Then, we moved a little bungalow that was on our property and attached it to the primary structure to make a bathroom and laundry room. Later we added a 2 ½ car garage that was built from scratch — with the help of family members when it was needed. It didn't matter to us that as kids we seemed always to be working on something — we didn't know the difference. It unquestionably reinforced our work ethic, and we continued to learn about achieving satisfaction through hard work with visible results.

Our school was only 8 miles away. However, the bus ride took about 45 minutes each way because of the rural countryside. The school's name was Wallkill Central School. Until I graduated, I can count on my two hands the number of times I either drove to school or someone I knew drove and picked me up for the ride. The school bus was our transportation to and from school. Compare that to our children who never took a bus once they and their friends turned 16 and had a driver's license – Yes, times just changed. The students that played sports after school had a unique "sports bus" and that ride was not only longer, but it dropped me off a mile from my home so that I could walk the rest of the way and get some exercise - NOT. Contrary to what our parents told us, it wasn't uphill in both directions, and I didn't have to walk in the snow either!

Voting Polls

While we didn't feel exceptionally political in our home, we were acutely aware of elections, who was running in local elections and indeed the primary elections every two years. My dad sat on the school board, and my mother always worked at the voting polls during elections. Polling locations were at the local school, and my mother would go first thing in the morning and stay until late into the evening. It was a special day in our home for two reasons. My dad prepared dinner which was unusual, and it was something special plus we got to stay up late until our mom came home to give us a full report on the election results. Etched in my memory is the 1960 election. For a lot of reasons, this was an important election. As youngsters, we always knew General Eisenhower for obvious reasons in the post-WWII era. Ike had finished his two terms and his Vice President Richard Nixon was running against the young John F. Kennedy from Massachusetts, and there were a lot of public controversies. We watched the debates on our black and white television because we were starting to pay attention to election politics. My sisters were in their teens, and I was eleven. When my mother got home on election night, she sat down with all of us and, of course, my father was most interested. Mom told us that it seemed almost positive that Kennedy had won the election and my father was not too happy. She then told us two things that I distinctly. First, she said it was the first time in her life that she had voted for a Democrat for president. While we understood the difference between the political parties, my parents never told us who they voted for. They taught us that it was up to the individual to decide and they didn't want to influence us with their decisions. So, that was unusual for her to say and my father said that he had voted the other way. Second, she said that in her opinion, Kennedy would die in office because every 20 years the elected president dies in office. Look it up. Starting in 1840, every 20 years the U.S. elected president died in office. My mother was an avid reader and just knew that bit of history as being significant.

Prediction Realized

A vital feature of the first expansion to our original little house was a room dedicated as a dining room. It was not a formal affair, but it was beneficial, and a place where we did our homework after dinner until we each had our individual bedroom – well into our teens. My dad built a table from a solid core smooth door and used wrought iron legs. There were two benches on either side that could fit three people and on both ends, were captain's chairs with arms. All pieces were highly varnished in natural wood and when people who visited for the first time, they didn't know our dining room table wasn't store bought. Frankly, it didn't matter to us or anyone else. It was where we all sat each evening for dinner together. The most important part of the day was our dinner discussion, and it was imperative that we were home for – there was no allowance for being late for dinner time in our house.

The seating arrangement was Dad at the head and Mom to his left and closest to the kitchen. I got the other end, and my two older sisters sat to my father's right and my youngest sister sat to my right. God forbid if you put your elbow on the table while we were eating. My dad was an Air Force officer, and there were strict rules about manners at the table, and they were clear. My parents first taught us the correct way to do things. Then, they reminded us when we strayed. Then, when we knew better, they enforced the rules taught.

The evening I remember most sitting at that dinner table was the night of November 22, 1963. It was a Friday, and I was in the 9th grade. As we were getting onto the bus to go home, the word started to spread that President Kennedy got shot. Of course, we had no idea that he was not in Washington D.C. since there was no such thing as morning news programs. When we got home, we found out the terrible details. I remember it like yesterday, and it's still difficult for me to talk about because of the emotion I feel to this day. Recently, while I was watching the movie *Jackie* with Natalie Portman, there were times I just had to pause the video to gather myself. It was a tough time in our country's history for sure, and it's an emotional subject for those of us that lived through the assassination of our President.

The night President Kennedy died, we had guests for dinner at our dining room table. My Aunt Gussie and Uncle Otto were scheduled to eat Friday night dinner with us. We regularly attended church, but not overly religious and said grace on holidays, but not every night before dinner. On this occasion, my dad said: "let's say grace tonight." He proceeded to ask the blessing, and it was the first time I'd seen my father unable to speak because he was crying so hard. It made such an impression that I cannot even write about this event without getting a little choked up myself. For those of us who lived through this period, it is easy to understand that there are still new movies and books being released now over 50 years after President Kennedy's assassination. Two days later on Sunday morning, we watched Jack Ruby kill Lee Harvey Oswald in the basement of the Dallas jail live on the black and white telecast and could not believe it was happening. What a tragic time in our country's history.

Final Construction Project

My most memorable accomplishment with my father is the last project we did together. It was a beautiful barn, actually a workshop, which we built together starting in 1967 during my last year living at my parents' home and it took several years for us to finally complete. We hired someone to dig the footings with a backhoe, but from then on, it was all our labor – with a little help from our friends and family members when extra hands were needed. We mixed the concrete ourselves and poured the footings. We put in the block foundation entirely by ourselves, and I learned the technique of laying cement blocks and did my fair share. Then, we built the first story frame with the help of a big group my uncles and completed it in one weekend. My Uncle Ray was an expert at framing, so he was always the head boss of that process in every framing job we did including this one. My dad and I built all of the gambrel trusses and then had the family team come back for a Sunday of raising the roof. The entire outside surface, including the roof, was finished with tongue and groove rough cut pine. The front half of the barn was open from floor to roof peak, and the back half had a partial second story for storage. We completed our barn in 1970, and the delay was significant due to other interruptions that weren't anticipated and were unpreventable. This photo has been hanging in my office since my mom gave it to me as a housewarming gift in 1984. My dad passed away in 1979 at the unbelievably young age of 59. You can imagine the mental image I have each time I look at this photograph. Once completed, it was a work of art created primarily with two sets of hands and two brains working together.

Our barn was finally completed in 1970. The project was interrupted by my Dad's unexpected call to active duty and my education at Kings Point. The results were worth the wait!

Making the Decision - USMMA Kings Point

Where I grew up, seven miles from our home was Stewart Air Force

Base which was extremely active in the 1950s and 1960s. It was primarily a base for supply operations and pilot training. My father remained in the Air Force Reserves throughout his life and didn't retire until after I was married and moved away from my boyhood home. We spent a lot of time at the Officer's Club on the base during my teenage years. There were swimming pools and tennis courts that we could use. Food and drink were unbelievably inexpensive, and it was the place my parents took us to eat out and for special holidays or celebrations. We were immersed in Air Force officers and their families throughout this experience. As an Officer's Club Member, my dad also had access to the Officer's Club on the West Point Post which was only twenty miles from our home. Because of the prestige and history of West Point, it was a terrific experience for us to go there, walk around the grounds, and have a lovely dinner for a special occasion.

At an unusually young age, probably around 12 or 13, I decided I wanted to enlist in the military and become a career officer by attending a Military Academy instead of going to a regular college and apply to an ROTC program to be an officer. I was an only son who was greatly influenced by my father and looking back; it surely makes sense. The process of applying to the U.S. service academies was complicated and hard work. There were ongoing physicals, interviews, tests and then more of the same. Since I applied for entrance to more than one service academy, I had to repeat the procedure several times. To become a candidate, the first step was to send a formal letter of application to your US Congressman and two US Senators for a nomination. I applied to three of the four US service academies plus the US Coast Guard Academy which did not require a congressional nomination. The USCG Academy needed a direct application, and they demanded a separate physical, interview, and other application procedures. Each US Congressman and each US Senator was allotted five nominations to each of the four service academies, and then each Academy made the final decision. Over time, a lot of the nomination and appointment procedures changed, but this was how it worked during my applications for nomination. My mom was exceptionally well organized and is the one I credit most for my final success of achieving an appointment before my senior year in high school even got started.

During the yearlong application process, my oldest sister was dating and eventually married a young Air Force First Lieutenant stationed at Stewart Air Force Base close to our home. There was a point in this process where a decision was needed. I was 1 of 5 nominees for the Air Force Academy but was not accepted by the Academy yet. I received a Congressional nomination, and I was selected by the U.S. Merchant Marine Academy in Kings Point, NY. My problem was that I'd worn glasses starting around fourteen for distance vision and my depth perception was a problem due to astigmatism. The bottom line was that I would never be a jet pilot in the Air Force. Here I was in the summer after my junior year of high school and faced with a decision that would affect my life. I asked my future brother-in-law, Jerry, who was on active duty in the Air Force what he suggested. He recommended I look at life after graduation and where the long-term rewards after I fulfilled my obligation, would be best for my goals. Hands down, that was at Kings Point, and that's how I ended up accepting an appointment to the US Merchant Marine Academy in Kings Point, New York.

Published Requirements for Admission to Kings Point:

In addition to requiring strong GPA and SAT/ACT scores, to be eligible to enter the Academy a candidate must:

- Be of good moral character.
- Be at least 17 years of age and must not have passed his or her 25th birthday before July 1 in the year of entrance.
- Be a citizen of the United States either by birth or naturalization, except for a limited number of international midshipmen specially authorized by Congress.
- Meet the physical, security and character requirements necessary for appointment as Midshipman in the U.S. Naval Reserve.
- Obtain a Congressional nomination to the Academy from a Member of Congress.
- Submit a completed application; and
- Qualify scholastically.

Medical/Physical Clearance – Candidates are required to pass a DoD-

MERB (Department of Defense Medical Examination Review Board) physical, and take the Candidate Fitness Assessment (CFA) to assess physical fitness.

Security Clearance – to receive a commission at graduation as an officer in the U.S. Armed Forces, candidates are required to complete security clearance paperwork while at the Academy to qualify for a security clearance upon graduation.

My high school friends were just starting to think about which clothes they would pack and take with them before heading to their freshman year of college. They still had another month or six weeks to do their planning. In mid-July, I had the one bag I was allowed to carry all packed with my allowed essentials. While my buddies still had their feet up, I had already begun the "hell" known as plebe year at any US service academy. We routinely referred to Kings Point or USMMA as the forgotten federal Academy because we were smaller in size and received less publicity. All of the rights of passage and military obligations after graduation applied to Kings Point as with West Point, Annapolis, and the Air Force Academy. We were obligated to stay in the service as an active US Navy Reservist with all of its commitments and actively work on a U.S. Flag merchant vessel for a minimum of 3 years. We had to remain a Naval Reservist for a total of 6 years after graduation. There were two other options available to fulfill our obligation. We could elect to accept a full-time active duty position in either the Marines or Navy for a minimum period of 3 years.

Chapter 2
Learning the Kings Point Way
Plebe Year

Being a Plebe

Upon arrival at the Academy, we were instructed to say our goodbyes to our folks and friends and immediately go to Bowditch Hall Auditorium for a welcome address by the Regimental Officer. This very sharp clean-cut man, who had to be forty-something, stood at the podium. As I later had to memorize, Captain O'Leary was the Regimental Officer in charge of the entire regiment of midshipmen. We sat in our "street clothes" for the last time until we left the Academy either on graduation day or before. We listened with anticipation, and I only remember one thing he said in his address to the 325 plebe candidates sitting in a hot and stuffy room in the heat of the summer. "Look to your left and then look to your right. Those two people you looked at won't be here on graduation day." The dropout rate for the previous year's graduating class from starting day to graduation was 66%. We were beginning our Academy career in 1967 and, if we could make it, we would graduate in 1971. If you couldn't handle the pressure of making the grades or survive the strict regimentation, you'll leave before graduation time. Our class of 1971 was either extremely lucky or maybe just better prepared. Four years later, we only lost about 1/3 of our members, and 221 of us got to toss our hats in the air.

After Captain O'Leary's "inspirational" address, we were immediately hustled off to muster up in Barney Square to begin our first day of indoctrination. It was already clear before we arrived that it was the last time we'd be smelling freedom until our first leave at Thanksgiving over four months away. A couple of uniformed officers stood in front of the mass of young civilians and called our name. A 3rd classman, one of the few on the square dressed in uniform, told us to "fall in" and thus began our plebe indoctrination. We looked like a bunch of wandering minstrels dressed in our shirts and ties and jackets and a single suitcase in our hand. Not knowing a left from right and sweating like pigs already, screams from the upperclassmen were already reverberating off the brick Academy building walls. Little did we know that they wouldn't stop their yelling for a very long time. My section number was 328, and we were led off to 6th company, Jones Hall, and told to take our bag to our room and get back outside at once. There were 28 of us in section 328 beginning that first day of Academy life.

NEWS ⊞ LONG ISLAND

For Daily Home Delivery Call Nassau 433-1220 Suffolk 543-4141

DAILY NEWS, MONDAY, JULY 31, 1967   27

Roll Call at the Academy

"Will you please step forward as I call your name." These are plebes about to be assigned to quarters at the U.S. Merchant Marine Academy at Kings Point. The new class includes men from the 50 states as well as Puerto Rico and the Canal Zone. Classes start next Monday.

A couple of weeks after we reported for indoctrination, the local paper ran this cover.

As we ran outside to form up again, we found the guy who marched us off was called our "Pusher," and he was a 3rd classman. We were off to get our first issue of clothing – sneakers, socks, gym shorts and a tee shirt. After returning to strip down and put on our new "uniform," we said goodbye to our civilian clothes and our bags were headed for a common baggage locker to be forgotten for a very long time. With our tee shirts tucked in and all dressed the same, our pusher was now ready to start making us march in formation. We headed immediately to get a nice head shave at the barbershop. The "Pusher's" job was to teach his assigned section of plebe candidates everything they needed to know. That included the proper way to wear a uniform, when and how to salute, how to shine shoes and belt buckles, orientation for carrying out cleaning duties in the barracks and all things that went into being a "squared away" midshipman. It became evident that Pusher was a perfect name for his duties. Kings Point was the first of the federal service academies to open enrollment to women, but that was in 1974, seven years away.

There was a speaker system in our company — very much like those we had in our school growing up. Whenever we heard an announcement, it began with "Now hear this, now hear this." It ended with "That is all." We had to stop whatever we were doing and listen without talking. If caught in the hall — we were instructed to freeze, hit the wall, brace, and pay attention. These were announcements in the barracks hall we lived in, but there was another system that sounded throughout the entire Academy and everyone, everywhere stopped to listen.

There was no talking at all anywhere, anytime except when we were inside our room. Fear of the unknown was prevalent. So far, I had barely had time to meet my newly appointed roommate, Mike, who didn't get to toss his hat in the air at the end. Our assigned room was 6105, and it was time to learn how to make our beds (forever after "rack") properly. That was our assignment until dinner — or as we learned to call it — "chow." Inside our 6th company barracks were two sections of young new plebes in gym shorts and tee shirts and a group of upperclassmen yet to be identified, but they sure looked scary. We learned that this smattering of upperclassmen was our company's 1st class officers and a group of 2nd and 3rd classmen that were present to indoctrinate the new plebe candidates. It was hot and steamy that first afternoon, and I discovered my new roommate had not used a sufficient amount of deodorant that morning. A 2nd classman came into our room, and we stood up but had no idea what to do or say. He quickly set us straight on the proper reaction when an upperclassman arrives and how to "sound off" and then what the word brace meant. Bracing is an exaggerated form of attention with your head held high and pulled back and tucked down so you could produce a few wrinkles under your chin. The upperclassman will follow up with "Mister" and 14 various cuss words that were not kind to either your mother or your sister and positively not you, the turd, who just arrived to ruin their, otherwise, pleasant day.

The not so nice 2nd classman was there to show us how to make our rack and to inform us that we would not be climbing inside the covers for the next year, but would, instead, be sleeping on top of the correctly made rack. There was an additional heavy wool blanket perfectly folded at the foot of the rack, and that was what we'd be sleeping under for the next year. He explained how we'd be walking starting the very next time we left our room. We would be in a full brace position 6 inches from the wall (forever after called a "bulkhead"), and each corner we reached had to be "squared off." When you were outside, there was no walking, only jogging. But, don't think you could run however you want, MISTER! We had to learn the proper way to double time. As our first dinner was approaching, it was getting progressively louder both inside the barracks and outside along the paths around the Academy. Everyone looked goofy in their shorts, white socks and sneakers trying to double time with upperclassmen yelling in their face. Oh, yeah, I would be looking just as goofy and sweating and bracing and throwing back "yes sir" and "no sir" because that's all we knew on day one in our new home called Kings Point.

Immediately following chow that first day, we had not yet been exposed to "plebe knowledge" and knew very little except our names. Instead of having a post-evening chow plebe beat, they lined the plebe candidates from Jones Hall up in the parking lot, and we did wind sprints to see who was the last guy standing that wasn't vomiting and dry heaving. It was our indoctrination into that fear that followed each evening meal that you might not keep that food you just ate down or, at the very least, it won't be pleasantly digested.

At 2200 that first night we heard "Taps" sound for the first time. Lights went out, and when our heads went down, there was nothing until reveille sounded the following morning at 0600 and scared the shit out of us. Our day began with being assigned cleaning station duty and our first 50 minutes before morning chow was spent learning how to clean those places in the barracks that only a plebe could learn to clean properly. After breakfast, we did more cleaning and then had our first muster for colors on the "Oval." This day began our first "issue" of materials that continued in a steady stream over a two-week period.

Materials included everything we needed for our life as a midshipman. It started with a little book named Bearings. This little 225-page book formed the basis that would become known to all plebe candidates as "plebe knowledge." There were details about every single location in and around the Academy grounds. Eventually, we needed to know each word in this little blue book and spew it from our lips on command by every upperclassman that demanded to know what we knew. Also, we needed to provide the name of every regimental, battalion and company midshipman officer. On every desk in each room throughout the Academy, there was a loose-leaf binder entitled Kings Point Regulations. We had to learn a vast amount of that book's contents as it would control the majority of our lives over the next four years. Every spare minute we had available had to be spent learning our plebe knowledge, and before long, we'd find out why.

The little blue book of plebe knowledge was our Bible and nearly every word had to be committed to memory.

The regiment was made up of 6 companies, each with their name. 1st Company - Palmer Hall, 2nd Company - Murphy Hall, 3rd Company – Cleveland Hall, 4th Company – Rogers Hall, 5th Company – Barry Hall, and 6th Company – Jones Hall. Every building throughout the Academy had a name, and we were required to know the name and the history of the person the building was named after. Each of the company barracks was 3 decks high. Each company had a group of midshipmen officers that ran the company. There were 3 battalions each made up of 2 companies. There was a group of midshipmen officers that ran each battalion. While we got indoctrinated for 3 weeks, there were 325 plebe candidates and about 60 or 70 upperclassmen tasked with the duty of indoctrinating the plebe candidates. Once the entire regiment returned to prepare for classes, there were approximately 125 midshipmen in each company. Another 150 midshipmen were participating in their sea year duties and were not in residence at the Academy.

The living area of Kings Point where we lived, ate, did laundry, and, on occasion, relaxed at the canteen, was shaped like a "U" and the buildings interconnected by both the main deck and also by an underground basement called "zero deck." Each leg of the U was our 6-company barracks and located at the bottom loop, was Delano Hall which also housed a lower level lounge and canteen. The zero deck was a convenient way to get around the living areas, especially during inclement weather. It was also the site of some of the worst activities we experienced – Plebe Beats.

We spent our first day or two getting measured and receiving our first issue of uniforms and then instructions how to properly wear them. We received a plebe knife that we carried in our pocket at all times along with change for a quarter and a handkerchief. Do NOT be caught without any of those 3 "plebe gear" items or there'd be hell to pay, and you could find yourself walking tours on Barney Square with the M-1 rifle you just received and now hung on a couple of wire hangers under the rack that you couldn't lay on. Oh, this is going to be a lot of fun. So much to learn and we were just getting started!

A plebe was not allowed to have more than one additional plebe in the room – total 3 people maximum. I worked up enough courage the first couple of days to go next door and meet the two plebes that lived there. We were in a strange location on the 1st deck of Jones Hall with only two rooms isolated with another room at the end of a short hallway. We talked about the other room at the end of the hall and how busy and noisy it was, especially at night. It seemed like everybody was having fun, watching television and talking loud. It was the company wardroom and, while it was a place all upperclassmen were using, we found out that in the regular school year it was strictly for use by 1st classmen and no one else could enter except the plebes that were assigned to clean it for the week. So far, I had met about half of the other plebes who lived on my floor. A couple of them helped fill in some blanks for me so I could begin to understand what was going on around this place. My new friend, Sully, had already gone through this "hell" before. I asked, "What are you talking about? Why are you back?" It turns out there's a system for everything, and it needed to be added to the growing list of plebe knowledge, and it certainly helped to make sense of my new home at the Academy.

Some members of our plebe class carried the term "setback." That meant that the Academy officers who composed the boards of review for academics and discipline determined that the person they were preparing to expel had learned a valuable lesson and thus would be given an opportunity to return the following year to try plebe year all over again. The term "setback" was synonymous with a repeat of a previous year. While it could happen during any of the four years at King Point, it was most common to be a setback to repeat the plebe year. Anyone who chose to repeat the hell year of a plebe deserves all the respect in the world. My friend, Sully, did the unthinkable and elected to repeat his plebe year and he was our guide through the minefield as all of our section-mates learned, especially in the very beginning when none of us knew anything.

We soon learned about a few more important things. Classes would begin around the 2nd week of August, and the entire regiment would return about a week before that to get settled in before classes. Upperclassmen called us "plebe candidates," and our pusher told us that sometime during the first week of September there would be a special ceremony of "Acceptance." We would be sworn into the Navy Reserves and take our obligation oath. At that point, we would be full-fledged plebes. Don't dare confuse this with being 4th classmen because that was still a long way off. If you're lucky, you might be a 4th classman sometime in April or May next year. Wonderful! We're still nine months from being on the bottom rung of the ladder!

One of many pieces of plebe knowledge we had to learn was to know word-for-word what was on the menu for the next meal. We stood at a bulletin board where the meals got posted on a printed mimeographed sheet of paper and with our little notepad wrote the meal down precisely so we could return to our room to memorize it. Whenever an upperclassman approached and addressed us, we hit the bulkhead in a full brace and then sound off –

"Sir, Midshipman Jockers, sir!"

"Mr. Jockers, do you know what we'll be having today for lunch?"

"Sir, yes sir."

"What are you waiting for you fucking asshole? Tell me what's for lunch!"

"Sir, for lunch today we will have a salad with French dressing. Hamburgers on a toasted bun with tomatoes, lettuce, and pickles. French fried potatoes. String beans with roasted almonds. Chocolate cake with vanilla icing and nuts. Milk, water, and bug juice. Sir!"

The menu got regurgitated to the upperclassman as posted on the bulletin board - precisely. The advantage, we learned much later was eventually the menu repeated later in the month. Also, there were particular sections always the same – like milk, water and bug juice for lunch. Since this was early in our days of plebe knowledge, it took some time to memorize the exact menu items that were all new. Our buddy, Sully, could nail it every time while we stumbled our way through it and then upperclassman got pissed off and started asking for more plebe knowledge like – "What are the names of the paths to get from Samuel Hall to Barry Hall, Mister?"

Before each muster for chow, there was a beeper system that got blasted over the intercom throughout the Academy buildings and grounds. 5 beeps sounded 5 minutes before muster and 1 less beep each minute until the bugle call to muster sounded. There was paperwork and standard forms to be learned along with their, accepted nicknames. We were subjected to a whole new language of terminology. Discipline was undoubtedly the first thing to learn since it was the most painful. Receiving a form RO-30 from an upperclassman to walk tours hurt badly. Receiving a form RO-8 to perform extra duty hurt even worse! The slang term was that you'd been "stuck" - and you were!

A plebe was assigned to each floor in every company to sound off the menu for chow and announce throughout the regiment how much time remained before muster. Plebes were assigned this job for a week and performed it 3 times per day. Several minutes before the beepers started going off, you had to be at our announcement station and ready to begin. Breakfast at 0625, lunch at 1155 and dinner at 1825. At the appointed time, 5 beepers sounded you said - "Sir, there are now 5 minutes to morning chow. For this morning's chow, there will be orange juice, soft boiled eggs...." the exact posted menu items on the bulletin board. One minute later, 4 beepers sounded, "Sir, there are now 4 minutes to morning chow. For this morning's...." All plebes were required to be outside at the company muster station standing at attention before 3 beepers sounded. Upperclassmen could arrive anytime before the bugle sounded the call to muster. The plebes who were announcing the menus left their position after the final announcement with 1 minute remaining and had the liberty of walking inside through the company main decks to Delano Hall for mess.

The entire regiment was in formation on paths outside their company in two platoons for each company, and we marched to Barney Square in front of the mess hall, Delano Hall. As we climbed the stairs by platoon, the platoon leader gave the command to uncover, and simultaneously we removed our caps before entering the mess hall. Probably this would be impressive to watch as an outsider for 750 people to enter the dining hall and be ready to take seats before chow in 5 minutes or less, for us, it was just more routine, and it felt like a herd of cattle headed for the barn and not a military activity. The Midshipman Officer of the Day (MOD) stood at a podium on the raised stage where the regimental staff was seated for chow. Before each meal, the MOD turned on a mic and announced: "at ease." He said grace and then said – "Take seats." Thus, went our chow formations three times every day except Sunday.

Plebe Beats

On our second night as a plebe candidate, right after dinner, an announcement was made for all plebe candidates to muster on the zero deck immediately. This was to be our first of the nightly rituals following evening mess called a "plebe beat." It was exactly what it sounds like. There were about 50 plebes in 6th company, and we lined up in a brace

against a single bulkhead on the zero deck, and upperclassmen proceeded to beat us. Not physically, but verbally. They were not allowed
to hit us, but we might end up doing pushups or other physical challenges.
During our indoctrination period, our plebe beats lasted 45 minutes to an
hour. When the beat was over, we were soaking wet with sweat, and
even the upperclassmen needed to shower afterward. Few places had
air conditioning, and positively, there was none on the zero deck. Hot
water pipes were running overhead along the zero deck just to keep
things toasty warm for us! There could be vomit involved and, in some
situations, crying. Our responsibility was our plebe knowledge. In the
beginning, we didn't have the right sequence of knowledge to properly
answer or had forgotten altogether, and that's how it progressively got
worse. Upperclassmen would hand out RO-30's, each involving an hour
of walking tours on Barney Square like they were Halloween candy. You
could also easily find yourself reporting to an upperclassman's room at
0555 and standing there in full uniform waiting until reveille at 0600.
Then, knock on the door so that he could drill you on the knowledge you
previously answered incorrectly and then he'd go after more things you
didn't know. It was a slippery slope and one you could only recover from
by knowing all of your required plebe knowledge. Plebes got scrutinized
for their physical appearance, and a problem could always be found. Everything better be perfect: Spitshine on your shoes, cap brim no fingerprints, top of your cap tight enough to bounce a coin, belt buckle
gleaming and no fingerprints, collar insignias correctly placed, and the list
went on. He might even check to see if your underwear was stenciled
correctly, with your name in the requisite block letters!

Plebe beats on zero deck were held almost every night during the
week and continued until sometime in the 1st quarter of the following
year – around February or March. As long as some of the group of plebes
in our company did not have their shit together, plebe beats continued.
Overall bearing, dress, shoes, and plebe knowledge all determined the
level of beating you took. We learned to help those who fell short to get
our entire company of plebes in line and perfect. Eventually, the upperclassmen were satisfied with the results of their efforts and the plebe
beats became less frequent, though not eliminated until our Recognition

took place in April of our plebe year.

On our first Sunday, they told us we could attend church if we elected to. Suddenly, we all found religion! It was an opportunity to go somewhere that was air-conditioned, and we could avoid the upperclassmen that had evolved into non-stop harassment. We sat down and almost immediately nodded off. Church looked a lot more like a sleep-in than a religious service. It sure felt great to have an hour off.

Our Rooms

Our indoctrination included how to care for our room the "Kings Point way." Each room was identical. Two metal frame beds with a mattress on coil springs and your M-1 rifle hanging by hooks on the rack frame. A desk in the middle of the room with two armless wood chairs. On top of the desk was a dark blue regulation book and nothing else was allowed out in site when no one was in the room. Two sinks with a brass connecting drain pipe and mirrors above each sink. Two sets of lockers each with two doors and combination locks on each door – a total of four locks. The locker sets opened like French doors outward into the room. On the bottom half of each locker set were 8 wood faced drawers and on the top, were 6 cubbies. Each roommate had a full set of lockers. There was a single shared wardrobe locker and overhead doors above the lockers and wardrobe locker. A single metal trash basket that was not allowed to have any trash in it. Floors were dark brown vinyl tile. The door had a transom above it and there was a steam radiator for heat. Two windows that opened both top and bottom and a roller blind on each window. The 1st, 2nd and 3rd classmen could have a stereo system on the desk on the top furthest from the door. 1st classmen had cushioned armchairs.

One would assume this would be a pretty easy room to care for and keep clean. In actuality, absolutely everything had to be in a designated place and a specific configuration. Each drawer had a special use, and there was no allowance for deviation. Books had to be organized at the end of the desk in a certain order. Virtually everything had to be ink stenciled with your surname and class year. Preparing the room for inspection on Saturday is one thing. However, a plebe's room had to be inspection ready except for access to the combination lockers anytime you were not in the room. Also, the room's door could not be closed if you weren't in your room. A first-class midshipman officer or an Academy Officer could easily enter your room, inspect it, and give you an RO-8 with demerits for any offense.

We were taught by our pusher and the upperclassmen that were present for our indoctrination how to organize our room, and we had diagrams to follow proper organization requirements. We were also introduced to a device called a hand buffer. It was a heavy metal object that weighed about 25 pounds. The base was 1 foot long by 5 inches wide and 5 inches high with a stiff brush on the bottom. This object had a handle that was larger in diameter than a broom but about the same length. The handle had a hinge connection to the heavy metal base, and by moving the handle, the base could go back and forth, but not side to side. What did we use this strange heavy object for? To make that ugly brown tile floor gleam with a mirror finish using only Johnson paste wax. There was no substitute for Johnson Wax.

Our indoctrination instructors also taught us how to polish our brass belt buckle that held our web belt together so you could see your face in it. Brasso became our close, personal friend. It was also used to polish and shine the brass pipe that ran between the two sinks, so it gleamed. They taught us to spit shine our black plastic corfam shoes and the proper way to roll our clothes so we could store them in the right drawer location. Preparing our rooms so they could pass inspection whether present or absent became an art form in itself. There were things you learned to do to avoid making a mess that would later add more work. In those first weeks, you might return to your room to find it turned upside down with books thrown everywhere and your rack torn about and the medicine cabinets emptied into the sinks. A note on the desk informed you about the punishment for the offense of leaving your room in less than perfect condition.

Throughout our entire Academy life, we were allowed to have one box in our personal locker called a "personal box." There was nothing else in our possessions that couldn't be touched or inspected. This personal box was off limits to everyone including upperclassmen and even the Academy staff officers. Everything else we owned or were assigned was open season to anyone once your lockers were unlocked.

Mess Duty

Part of our most essential training lessons involved food in the mess hall. During our first week or two, we attended a class with our section mates to learn about military etiquette. For several days, we had a visiting instructor who taught us the proper way to set the table, how to eat like a gentleman and not a slob, proper etiquette in the company of a lady, all things that related to conducting yourself as an officer and a gentleman at all times. It did not take long before upperclassmen were drumming the rules of proper etiquette into our heads.

Our next pusher training was to learn how to work in the mess hall and serve food. The plebes throughout the regiment were assigned by section to work together on food service. Luckily, I had worked serving food at special public events that were related to the Masons and Eastern Star which my parents had been active in while I was growing up. I had already learned from my mother how to properly set a table including multiple forks and knives depending on what was being served. Since my mom worked when I was young, my sisters and I had assigned duties, and it was second nature to conduct myself appropriately when around food service. Mess hall service was a massive scale, but at least I wasn't starting with zero experience.

While there were only about 400 people to serve during our indoctrination, we were learning how to prepare the tables and serve food when there would be twice that many people at each meal. Thirty minutes before the meal began, our section arrived at the mess hall. Each table held nine people, and the server stood at the foot of the table at parade rest. There was an elevated dais for the regimental midshipman officers, Academy officers joining us, and any special visiting guests. The head table sat about 25 people. Sometimes the dais was full during the year, but during our indoctrination training, it was only about half full. There was a serving section from each of the six companies, and each of us had assigned tasks for service. We first had to set the tables — Tablecloths were changed daily, plates, glassware, utensils, napkins, and serving utensils were all prepared and clean from the previous meal and ready in the pantry area of the kitchen. Approximately 80 tables were set up, and each table was assigned to an individual plebe server for the day. We rotated the serving duty during the week to ease the pain of our section mates. That meant over the course of the year, you had mess duty every other week and served the food about once a month which was not too bad. It was not agonizing except on special occasions. During big events like homecoming weekend or holiday meals, we would have dress uniform dinners. Those were not the events you wanted to have the serving duty. However, on a Friday night in the fall before a home football game, there was a ton of spirit leading up to the big Saturday game, and we would have "crazy hat" dinner events. Indeed, that was the time to have the serving duty!

There weren't formal assigned seats for mess, but upperclassmen normally sat in the same place for each meal. Plebes served tables for the company where they lived. 1st classmen sat at the head, plebes were spread around at the foot of the table and 2nd and 3rd classmen were in the middle seats. As plebes, we had to sit forward in our seats and kept our eyes facing front unless we were addressed, there was no talking by plebes during meals. When the meal finished, plebes could not leave the table until excused by the head of the table. The plebe with serving duty had to run back to the kitchen with his tray to bring back the next serving. At dinner, there were 3 courses – soup or salad, main course, and dessert. When the table was empty, the mess hall duty sections would have to clear the tables and take all of the used dinnerware and serving dishes to the staging area in the kitchen for professional cleaning by the kitchen staff.

There were some creative eating habits and one we picked up as we reached our 1st class year. The group that I ate with during our 1st class year all liked toast for breakfast. There were two commercial grade toasters in the kitchen that held 3 or 4 slices of bread wide, and the continuous chain feed mechanism dropped 4 slices of toast about every 10 seconds. For breakfast, we would send our server plebe to the toaster and toast a complete loaf of bread and hurry back with a bag of toasted bread. If the server were busy getting food in the kitchen, we would assign the task to another plebe sitting at the foot of our table. Habits we learned by experience and adopted as our own!

Company Officers and Other Staff

Located at each company barracks on the main deck near one of the entry doors from the outside was a company office. The company office is where mail arrived, and we had to ask the upperclassman on watch or his assistant, always a plebe, if they had any mail for you. It was from this company office that company-wide loudspeaker announcements originated. There was a second office across the hall, and it was for either the Company Officer or the Battalion Officer. These were senior Naval officers or USMS (US Maritime Service) Officers. Often, they were Kings Point graduates in their late 20s or early 30s. However, sometimes they were older and crustier officers that routinely had a less than friendly disposition. They were mainly present to advise the Midshipmen staff officers and provide assistance if needed, which was rare. For the most part, they worked during the day and then went home at night, but it seemed like there was always at least one hanging around even at night.

Apparently out of boredom, sometimes they would wander around the company barracks and look for trouble especially in our rooms. Sometimes you'd return after class to find a little note including an RO-8 for having something wrong inside your room. A lovely gift from the Officer that got bored. When we were 2nd classman, we had one of the crusty old Battalion Officers whose name was Commander Meyer. He was from somewhere in the south, and we all called him "Beau Meyer." My roommate, Tom, and I had a newspaper rolled up and torn to simulate a Christmas tree taped to the outside of our door. One of our trouble making friends stopped by to visit when we weren't in our room. To let us know he stopped by, he lit the newspaper Christmas tree and let it burn. Upon our return, Tom and I met Beau Meyer standing at our door with the smoldering paper tree, and he exclaimed, "Someone's been fuckin' with your door, boy!!" The fear we had immediately was that crusty ol' Beau would restrict us during Christmas leave, and we'd be stuck sitting out our cherished leave restricted to Kings Point. It didn't happen, and we just had to clean our door. There was definite payback due for our friend who was the fire causing culprit.

By the end of our second week of indoctrination, I had met and even spent some time with each of the guys who were in my section. Each company had two sections of plebes, and each section had 25 to 30 mid-shipmen. Before we arrived at Kings Point, we had to choose our field of study. We could either study engineering which focused on the engine room operation of ocean-going vessels of both steam and diesel propulsion plants. Or, we could study the operation and maintenance of the entire ship including navigation, safety, loading and unloading cargo, and nautical science. Each company was made up of a section of plebes for each field of study. The nautical science group was called "deckies," and the engineering group was called "engineers." There was one group that only existed at Kings Point for a few years, and that studied both fields, and they were called "dualies." Companies 1 through 5 each had a section group of deckies and engineers. Our 6th company had a section of engineers and a section of dualies. The plebe sections lived on the 1st deck and the less desirable rooms on the 2nd deck. 2nd and 3rd classmen lived on the 2nd deck and the less desirable rooms on the 3rd deck. 1st Classmen lived on the 3rd deck almost exclusively. The exceptions were the top midshipmen officers, including the regimental midshipman staff officers, who all lived in 1st company. The company commanders and ex-ecutive officers had special rooms on the 1st deck with extra space be-cause of their added responsibilities. Also, the battalion commanders and battalion executive officers lived on the 1st deck in special rooms.

The individuals in your section were your classmates for plebe year, but they were much more than that. You lived and even played together for nearly 11 months. These were the worst of days and the best of days, and you spent them with this group of friends. Although you left most of your section mates after plebe year, most of them became your core group of friends through the rest of your time at the Academy and then long after. Most them are still good friends you just don't happen to see too much. During this indoctrination period, it was enough to know that there were guys right down the hall that were undergoing the same tests of character and intestinal fortitude to stick with it until things eventually got better. Once in a while in the early days, we'd go to the other's room or maybe go somewhere to have a coke just to get to know each other. More often we had to work together to clean an assigned cleaning station or help the other guy learn to spit shine something. As relationships grew during our plebe year, close relationships formed and brotherhoods evolved.

M-1 Rifles

One of our indoctrinators was a member of the drill team, and it was his job to teach us the manual of arms with our WWII vintage M-1 rifles. We would need to carry these rifles in parades, and we needed to be proficient at the basic manual of arms. It wasn't necessary to learn how to be a drill team level performer, only to march and salute properly using a rifle. When it was time to march in our first parade on a Saturday morning, we were ready to go with the rest of the regiment.

Return of the Regiment

As the end of the first week of August approached, it was our third week of indoctrination, and we were already starting to learn our position as plebe candidates. Now, another unknown was fast approaching, and there was a lot of discussion and preparation for the return of the upperclassmen when the Academy would fill up. Though we felt a foreboding, we had learned a lot in a rather short period. We gained some experience serving food and bracing as needed along with other duties that plebes were assigned. What we feared most was the impact of having so many upperclassmen at plebe beats and just generally giving us a hard time. It was mainly fear of the unknown and the realization that soon there would many more opportunities to get stuck by upperclassmen. All we could do is practice and prepare our plebe knowledge and avoid unnecessary contact with upperclassmen. In other words, learn how to hide.

The first group to return to the Academy on Saturday were the 2nd and 3rd classmen. Another thing we knew, but couldn't figure out was that our 2nd year (our 3rd class year) would be spent at sea on merchant vessels and, since many of our classmates played team sports, how would that work? About 1/3 or less of our class played a varsity team sport. The rest of us would go to sea for our entire 3rd class year. The sportsmen would split their sea year into two years instead of just one. "A-Splits" played fall sports including football and soccer and winter or spring sports like baseball, basketball, wrestling, sailing, and rowing were "B-Splits". In our plebe section 328 with 22 plebes, 8 of them took a split sea year. The returning 3rd classmen we saw arriving in August had just finished their plebe year and planned to play soccer or football and start attending their second year of classes. The 2nd classmen coming back were all returning from sea. Either they were part of the non-splits or the "A-Splits" back for their second time. It was the ones returning from a year at sea that were the fascinating characters. Some had pretty long hair and seemed to be getting used to Academy life again after being gone an entire year since they left as plebes.

The second group back the following day were mainly 1st classmen returning from a summer break following their 2nd class year. Some, however, were "B-Splits" that had just completed their sea year. Either way, all 1st classmen had completed two full years of classes and finished with their sea year training, and they were all back to finish their final classes before graduation in about ten months.

Now that everyone was back, the full complement present was approximately 750 midshipmen. Two of my new section mates had brothers at the Academy. My friend, Jon, from Pittsburgh, had a brother who was a 1st classman. My other friend, Donnie, had two brothers. All three of them played football. His brother, Ronnie, was his twin and was also a plebe. His other brother was a 3rd classman and had just completed his plebe year and was back on an "A-Split" to play football. Having Jon and Ronnie in our section was pretty helpful. Also, the fact that we had brothers of our newly discovered section mate brethren would prove beneficial as the year wore on. The immediate impact of having about 750 midshipmen around was two-fold. We were overly concerned about a large number of upperclassmen beating on us at the same time. Also, it seemed a lot more crowded, and it was interesting to see the impact at musters, meals, and colors formation. At our company, 6th Company in Jones Hall, we were a little bit isolated. We were the last barracks building, and the closest building to us was O'Hara Hall, the gym. On the other side of our building was the football field and then Vickery gate. As it turned out, it was a pretty convenient location for many reasons as we discovered throughout our plebe year.

The responsibility of the 1st classmen was to manage everyday midshipmen life including setting all of the watch schedules for all classes, maintaining the military bearing of all midshipmen as well as running parades, events and all extracurricular activities related to our Academy life. The commissioned officers present were there to advise and guide the 1st class leaders and help prepare leaders in the 2nd class for the following year to take command. 2nd classmen and 3rd class splits were responsible for training, guiding, and disciplining the plebes. The second year of classes was, by far, the worst course load of the four years.

When classes began the 2nd week of August, we began to settle into a routine during the week. Wake up at 0600 and clean your assigned plebe cleaning station, muster for morning chow, muster for colors and go immediately to classes. 1130 morning classes are over and return to the company barracks to muster for lunch at 1155. Afternoon classes ended at 1600. We had free time to exercise, attend activity meetings, and the sports teams practiced. At 1825, we mustered for evening chow. Following evening chow at 1900, we had to muster on the zero deck for a 30-minute plebe beat. Next, we studied in our rooms until Taps at 2200 when we could go to bed or study until 2300.

Acceptance Day

Daily lives were highly regimented. It was required to read the posted information to find out what was scheduled so you could then be sure to be prepared to take the necessary action. One of the significant scheduled events was plebe Acceptance Day. It was slated for the first Saturday in September over Labor Day weekend. It was also a unique chance to have your family visit the Academy; however, there would be no leave granted until Thanksgiving. I was lucky that my home was only hours away and my parents and sisters would drive to attend the event. This event was the day we would graduate from being a plebe candidate to a full-blown plebe. It truly was a pretty big deal.

Preparations for Acceptance Day began as soon as the entire regiment was back because we started Saturday morning parades immediately following inspection. Parades were a pretty important part of each Saturday, weather permitting. The midshipmen officers were all new to their positions, and they were refining their parade responsibilities just as we plebes were. The officers wore swords and marched ahead of each company or battalion. Their commands were yelled out to keep everyone in proper position throughout the parade routine. As we passed the review-ing stand, companies got the "eyes right" command to face the reviewing stand in unison – a critical part of each parade. The regimental band had a fixed series of music they played for each stage of the parade. All 6 companies marched onto the field and formed in the center of Tomb Me-morial Field. We faced the reviewing stands and listened to the speakers. Finally, we were instructed to pass in review and, then there was a fixed pattern for marching past the reviewing stand.

The plebe candidate class had exceptional practice sessions because we would need to "ground arms" and leave the company formation. We had to form up near the bleachers with our right hand raised to take an oath. We were sworn into the US Merchant Marine Academy and also swore to accept a commission in the Naval Reserves upon graduation and serve the agreed upon period. Finally, our practice completed, and we were ready to attend our first public parade. The dress was mixed for this occasion with the regiment in formal dress C, and all plebes were wearing service dress whites which we fondly called our "ice cream suits."

I remember that it was one of those absolutely clear bright blue sky days. I was looking forward to seeing my family as were many of my classmates. Some of them lived too far from New York and would have to wait until Thanksgiving to see their family for the first time since we started this ordeal. My family was duly impressed and proud of me. It was interesting that we were allowed to bring our families into the bar-racks to see our sparse rooms that they'd heard so much about by letters and phone calls. I was also able to introduce my new brothers in arms to my family for the first time. It was a most exciting transition as young men starting a new service academy life. We were now officially plebes!

*Acceptance Day 1967 in service
dress white (ice cream suit).*

Cleaning Stations & Duty Assignments

Bathrooms and showers were all public, and there was virtually no privacy whatsoever. All barracks bathrooms, showers, floors, and everything you could see or touch was cleaned 100% by plebes. The exceptions were the classroom buildings, library, mess hall and other public buildings. Company midshipmen officers created and rotated job assignments for the plebes for the week from Monday through Sunday. Jobs were posted on the company bulletin board and starting Monday morning; you knew what your job assignments were for the week. Even if you had mess duty for the week, you would also have a cleaning station assignment or other responsibilities to go along with it. Every week when jobs got posted you hoped for the simplest tasks like laundry duty or the wardroom cleaning, but it could be you'd end up with heads or slop sink which was the worst. The "cleaning stations" each had a precise method to clean, and there were daily inspections by the midshipmen officers and company commissioned officers. If job performance was substandard, the punishment was entirely up to the inspector. Saturday morning inspections were especially critical.

Every floor in each barracks had a head, shower room, slop sink, and a trash locker. It's not what one expects to have to do when you're accepted to attend a military service academy. It's my guess, but I can't be certain, that these plebe duties are no longer carried out at Kings Point and probably none of the other service academies.

Laundry Duty – Of the 125 or so total midshipmen that lived in a company, approximately 50 of them were plebes and the rest upperclassmen. Underwear and socks were washed by each midshipman at his own cost and time. There were public washing machines and dryers on the zero deck below each company barracks for general use. All uniforms required professional cleaning, and usually, you would use 2 or 3 sets of uniforms per week and sometimes even more during the summer months. You couldn't wear a summer shirt more than two days and have it pass inspection if you were a plebe. We had two laundry bags that had to be kept in the overhead doors in our lockers. One was for you to wash and the other was to send out for professional cleaning. We'd fill out a paper form, put it inside the bag with our dirty uniforms and take it to a central drop location. There was only one drop off spot for the entire regiment. 2 or 3 days later, the clean, folded, freshly starched and boxed uniforms were in alphabetical cubbies in the central drop off location for pickup.

A lady we called Ma Rooney was always present in the pickup room to take care of any problems. She felt sorry to hear the sad stories, principally from the plebes, and she would give out cookies to help drown your sorrows. All plebes took care of dropping the bag of uniforms off for cleaning. One of the duty assignments for plebes was to go around each morning to pick up any dirty uniform laundry bags that upperclassmen put outside their room for pickup and delivery by a plebe to the main drop off location. It was just another thing to look forward to after you became an upperclassman! This was one of those cherry assignments you hoped for when the plebe assignments got posted.

The 1ˢᵗ Class Wardroom - Located on the main deck of every company was a special room for 1ˢᵗ classmen only called the wardroom. This was the 2ⁿᵈ best plebe cleaning station assignment to get with 1ˢᵗ given to picking up laundry bags. The wardroom could be a mess for the plebe to clean especially after a weekend, but the conditions were easy to work in. It was the only air-conditioned place in the barracks, and the TV was always on so you could watch and listen while you were working. There was a coffee maker urn and lots of trash and empty soda cans. A high percentage of 1ˢᵗ classmen smoked, and ashtrays had to be emptied and cleaned.

Slop Sink – This was the room where all mops, buckets, cleaning brushes, cleaning supplies and, of course, a sink to fill them with water was located. In an adjoining space, there were buffers. Some of them were hand buffers, and some were large electric buffers. Each floor had a slop sink, a head, a shower room with 8 heads and a trash locker. Since everyone cleaning had to use the tools and supplies from the slop sink to finish their job, the slop sink might be even worse than cleaning the heads! Everyone used the mops and equipment, so you had to complete the final cleanup process last. It could be a messy job, especially on Saturday morning when the entire floor was preparing for inspection. This particular cleaning station was my very least favorite. I would even prefer the job of cleaning heads. Once you finished the heads on Saturday morning before inspection, you could ordinarily keep people out until inspection was over.

Showers – This was an important cleaning station. They needed to be cleaned and dried out to avoid any buildup of mildew and prevent the spread of any foot fungus and other communal diseases. When showering we always wore shower clogs, but that wasn't foolproof. Next door, the slop sink had all of the necessary chemicals and tools needed for cleaning. In addition to the tiled floor, walls and ceiling there were towel racks to clean and windows and doors as well. Some midshipmen preferred a morning shower, and some showed at night. Maintaining cleanliness in all plebe assigned stations drew careful attention by all of the upperclassmen. If you did a poor job, you'd hear about it without fail.

Heads – This was probably the assignment that every plebe hated the most. It was always the worst on Mondays. Especially if it was a long weekend and a day or two passed without being cleaned. Sundays were a day off for everyone, including plebes. No stations got cleaned on Sundays. The urinals and toilets had to be cleaned using the tools and equipment located in the slop sink next door. Floors had to be mopped, and windows and doors cleaned and dusted. It was a dirty stinking job, and with luck, you didn't have that cleaning station more than a few times over the course of your plebe year.

Trash Lockers – This was a room about 10 feet square, and there was a stand made from pipes with a huge canvas bag hanging from the pipe stand. The fully loaded canvas bag might weigh several hundred pounds. You had to drag the bag down to the zero deck to a drop off area where the garbage collection company would pick it up for disposal. All garbage in the trash locker had to be kept off the floor and make sure all of the walls and floors were kept perfectly clean. It was a messy job and often dirty job.

You and your fellow plebes were cleaning up the mess that everyone else in the company created, and that was not fun. It was hard and tedious work. We learned quickly after having one of those jobs, to be very careful not to make a mess ourselves and make the life of our fellow plebe any worse than it already was. If you dropped something on the floor while emptying the garbage can from your room, you just bent down and picked it up, so your friend didn't have to do it when he was cleaning the trash locker. The same applied to all other facets of life in the communal areas. Pick up after yourself or your friend would have to pick up after you. And then you would have to pick up after him too! We all learned very quickly to watch out for the other plebes on your floor and in your barracks. There was also no hesitation to remind someone who did something unacceptable to make it right. The system of cleaning up after yourself progressed up the line as well. We found that even the upperclassmen were not slobs and were aware that making work unnecessarily for others was not acceptable. There are exceptions to all generalizations and this is no different. Often it also had something to do with post liberty hangovers and the amount of alcohol that might have been consumed while on liberty!

Demerit System of Punishment

The demerit system applied to all midshipmen in all classes and was the primary form of punishment. The rules and regulation along with the standards for punishment were on top of every single desk in each room of the Academy. There's never a question that you'll be assigned demerits if you do something wrong. In the very rare instance that you might have truthfully been falsely assigned a punishment and you have a legitimate excuse or alibi, there was a system to appeal. The form used to issue demerits was a Form RO-8, and those were things you tried to avoid. Only midshipmen officers were allowed to issue demerits to underclassmen or, in rare instances, to members of their own class. Any regular officer could issue demerits to any midshipman.

There was a formal system for notification and assignment of demerits. The most serious offenses carried a significant penalty. Some examples of offenses with the worst penalties were the destruction of property, absent without leave (AWOL), missing a mandatory formation like a parade, or missing or showing up late for a watch.

You almost always knew when you got caught a.k.a. "stuck" for an infraction, but you certainly knew when you had committed a serious infraction and would be facing significant repercussions. Sometimes an officer or a midshipman officer would inspect your room or your cleaning station assignment and find there are wrongdoings. They left an RO-8 form as a nice surprise for you either in your mailbox or on your desk to let you know you've been "stuck" or did a poor job on your assigned task.

Each week a summary of all RO-8's issued the previous week was posted on a Mast List that was hung prominently outside company office. All midshipmen who were placed on report the week before and the number of demerits they received for the infraction was posted and required reading for everyone in the company. The Company Officer determined the punishment based on regulations. If there any room for interpretation, you could bet he would take the most severe punishment. In addition to demerits, plebes were required to walk tours on Barney Square Saturday afternoon with your rifle in hand.

The maximum demerit allowance for a plebe was 300, 200 for 2nd classmen, and 150 for 1st classmen. If the demerits imposed exceeded the yearly quota, a midshipman got called to a special hearing before a board of Academy officers, and potentially expelled for disciplinary reasons. Plebes were stuck with demerits for a broad number of reasons and typically for dumb mistakes. Upperclassmen mainly got stuck for major offenses like not returning from liberty on time. If they were caught AWOL (Absent Without Leave) the penalty was exceptionally stiff including possible expulsion from the Academy.

Extra Duty or E.D.

Whenever your demerit allowance exceeded the minimum monthly allotment of 10 demerits, you were required to work 1 hour of extra duty per demerit until you worked off the excess. At 1600, each weekday or at a specified time on Saturday afternoon the E.D. recipients mustered before the MOD (Midshipman Officer of the Day) for E.D. assignment. The uniform for E.D. was dungarees, and there was a brief inspection. Duties commonly required the deep cleaning of some workstation and the task was ordinarily at the barracks where you lived, but it might be anyplace. Often you were assigned to clean, wax and buff one of the decks in the barracks. You worked for 2 hours on weekdays and 4 hours on Saturday until the excessive demerits were worked down to the maximum monthly allowance. Naturally, plebes were the chief recipient of extra duty punishment. However, I can remember a few upperclassmen that received a harsh penalty for a major offense assigned E.D. for months to work off their punishment of demerits.

Restriction

In addition to working extra duty, once you exceeded the monthly allowance of demerits, the additional penalty of loss of liberty and restriction to the Academy was imposed. The Company Commanding Officer imposed a bare minimum of 1-week restriction. The bigger the sentence, the more weeks of restriction to Academy grounds or loss of liberty inflicted. Serious infractions received the highest penalties. We all knew the importance to avoid the wrong side of any Academy Officers.

While on restriction to grounds, at unscheduled and spontaneous times, a muster would be called over the Academy-wide PA system for all restricted men from all classes to report to a designed location. Failure to attend the "restricted man" muster resulted in the offense of AWOL while restricted, and the disciplinary action was enormously severe.

Morning Company Announcements

Before morning chow, at approximately 0630 each morning, the Midshipman Company Officer of the Day would make announcements about company activities and any special regiment activities for the day. This included uniforms to be worn, scheduled times for activities for the regiment, and times to muster for any special events. The announcements were made over a speaker system or 1 MC that was only heard inside the company barracks. All announcements began with the words "Now hear this, now hear this."

If the day was a normal class schedule weekday of breakfast followed by colors and then classes all day, the announcement was quite simple. 'The uniform of the day is long sleeve working khakis and A Jackets. Muster for breakfast will be outside. Muster for Colors is at 0750. That is all.'

First Class Wardroom

Every ship has a wardroom that is only for use by the complement of ship's officers. All meals are eaten by the officers in the wardroom and, quite often, the group of ship officers is also referred to as the ship's "wardroom." At Kings Point, a specially designated wardroom at each company was for the exclusive use by the company's 1st classmen. No other classes were permitted inside the wardroom except the plebe that was assigned to clean it daily. Inside this room were a television, nice comfortable chairs and sofas, a refrigerator, a giant coffee maker, and the highly-coveted air conditioner. Frequently, it was a gathering place for the company 1st classmen before musters for chow and before other regimental events. It is one of the privileges that everyone looked forward to when they finally reached their 1st class year. Once I finally had the highly-anticipated opportunity, I spent almost no time inside the wardroom. As with many places around the Academy, the people who hung out in this unique place were not necessarily the people you associated with and preferred to avoid instead. That was just my personal preference once I finally had access to the 1st class Wardroom.

Inspection and Saturday Routine

The Saturday morning routine started out like any other day – the 0600 reveille was followed by morning chow, but after breakfast, the day was completely different. Saturday mornings included the weekly event of full inspection of all rooms and plebe cleaning stations, and it was almost always at 0900. One of the two plebes in each room was the designated Room Captain, and the other was assigned to a cleaning station. A deep cleaning of all cleaning stations was required, and the inspecting officers performed a "white glove" inspection and deficiencies were awarded an RO-8 with demerits commensurate with the shortcoming.

The Room Captain was responsible for the room, but both plebes would work at getting it ready for inspection and each was responsible for their personal locker spaces. Deficiencies and imperfections inside the room usually fell on the Room Captain along with any demerits rewarded to the room space.

Floors/decks were a particular focus both in the main barracks halls and individual rooms. Plebes that were assigned the cleaning station of "barracks floors" and had to get them polished very early in the morning so that the upperclassmen could use the electric buffers in their rooms. Just as your shoes and belt buckle had to be highly polished so did the floor in your room. Polishing and buffing became an art form taught to each plebe on day one, but it was one to perfect over your life at the Academy. Where there was an abundance of large, powerful electric buffers on each deck of each company, there was a pecking order for using them. Plebes NEVER used them unless they were buffing the main hallway decks. Plebes could only use the manual buffers for the deck in their room. The polishing system used to put a shine on the floor had very exact rules and failure to follow them or try to shortcut the formula resulted in less than perfection. Johnson paste wax was the only wax used. Plebes would first spread the wax by hand and let it dry. The stiff brush 25-pound hand buffer is first used to bring a medium shine. Then, we had to use a scrap piece of a wool blanket (highly collectible) under the buffer's brush to bring a high sheen to the ugly brown floors. Plebes were required to shine their floors each day while upperclassmen could get by with only shining for Saturday inspection. The pecking order always applied to the electric buffers with 1st classmen being given highest priority on Saturday mornings.

47

Upperclassmen could use electric buffers on their deck while plebes used only hand buffers. The room captain was responsible for any shortcomings during Saturday inspections.

The top midshipman officers in the regiment were called a "wedge" because it was the group of officers that marched in the lead positions during parades. The highest-ranking midshipmen officers formed a wedge shape at the lead of each company or group. In progression, lowest to the highest order of seniority were a company wedge, battalion wedge, and the regimental wedge. During Saturday morning inspections, the greatest fear for all plebes was to have their room inspected by one of the wedges. The most coveted alternative was an inspection by a low-ranking 1st classman officer accompanied by a second classman with a clipboard.

Inspections came in two distinct categories. A routine inspection was conducted by the 1st class officers and with the particular focus on the plebe's rooms and their cleaning stations. It began at 0900 Saturday morning, and everyone was dressed in fresh working uniforms for the season. All rooms are completely clean, dust free, organized according to regulation, lockers and overhead doors open. After cleaning stations got inspected, the plebe left his cleaning station and returned to his room to stand by with his roommate the Room Captain. Upon arrival of the inspecting officer and his assistant armed with a clipboard and a stack of RO-8 forms to issue for less than perfect performance, the Room Captain called the room to attention. He announces "Sir, Midshipman Jones, Room Captain, ready for inspection, Sir."

Both inspectors have on white gloves and begin the dissection of your room. The slightest amount of dust or dirt, even in the most remote areas, will result in the Room Captain getting an RO-8 and the applicable demerits. New, inexperienced plebes commonly ended the inspection with a thoroughly trashed room with incorrectly organized lockers and overhead storage spread all over the pretty shiny floor. Everything required a stencil with your name and class number. Books, underwear, and uniforms, all had to be suitably stenciled, and all underwear and non-uniform garments had to be tightly rolled, in their assigned drawer, and nothing folded. Sometimes it took us an hour or more to put everything back where it belonged after an inspection. We often found ourselves walking tours on Barney Square and on Extra Duty to work off demerits we received during the Saturday morning room and cleaning station inspections.

During routine inspections, the same procedure was followed by 2nd classmen for their room inspection. By the time we reached our 2nd class year, we knew how to pass inspections without incident. The 1st classmen had to have their rooms in tip-top condition, but they not required to be standing by in their rooms. Most 1st classmen were involved in the inspection process, and their rooms didn't get inspected – assumption was their rooms were perfect anyway.

In anticipation of the inspection of cleaning stations, the plebe stood at parade rest at his station until approached by the inspection team. He snapped to attention, stated his name and "Sir, Midshipman Smith, ready for inspection, sir." Cleaning station inspections were difficult. If you had a particularly hard job like a head or shower, the inspection process was exceptionally detailed, and you better know what you're doing or be prepared to get some demerits for all your hard work. The potential existed that the inspector will tell you to re-clean the station and he would return later to re-inspect it again.

The second category of inspection, less frequent, involved dignitary guests accompanying the wedges and other inspectors. These Saturday inspections, held in dress uniforms, were followed by a formal parade. Any 1st classmen not involved in the inspection process had to stand by in their rooms for these inspections. The plebes' rooms were less apt to get trashed accompanied by demerits because the midshipman officers didn't want to make the plebes look bad in front of the visiting guests.

Parades

Just as with inspections, there were two different levels of parades on Saturday morning – weather permitting. A routine parade day would be in a standard uniform like working khakis and, while they are still very formal and regimented, the reviewing stands on tomb field were sparsely filled and there might not be any speakers at the parade. As with all parades, the marching band and color guard led the formation. These were more to practice and stay sharp. During formal parades that were often in full dress uniform, there was a special air about the event, particularly on a pleasant fall day like before a football game. Homecoming weekend or a formal ceremony like during graduation, the reviewing stands would be packed. The look of the entire regiment in full dress uniform was extraordinary and impressive to the members of the reviewing stand and guests in the grandstands. Anyone who has ever seen a military service academy on parade will know precisely the feeling you get as an observer. However, as a participant, it's quite special too, no matter how many times you've participated. You're proud of how impressive the regiment looks when they're doing what they've done even 100 times. Anyone who hasn't seen a formal military academy parade should put it on their bucket list.

Full dress formal parades on special occasions were particularly impressive. When the weather was just perfect, the look from the grandstands was special.

Classes

A 12-week quarter (roughly the equivalent class load of a semester in college) was required for 2 ¾ years of classes. A total of 11 quarters of courses to complete our BS degree in the selected field of study in Engineering or Nautical Science. As a result, the second full year of studies included as many as 27 credit hours during a given quarter. The class load didn't provide room for the study of basket weaving or pottery. Instead, we had those fun classes like thermodynamics, advanced calculus, and strength of materials along and all of the appropriate lab work. We were also required to study a language for 20 credit hours.

Yes, the numbers seem a little strange. We spent one full year at sea or a total of 4 quarters without formal classes. Then, in our 1st class year, we only had 3 quarters of classes. The final quarter was spent preparing to take a U.S. Coast Guard test for 3rd Assistant Engineer or 3rd Mate licenses – except the dualies who took both! This exam lasted one week (5 days) at 8 hours per day for a total test period of 40 hours. It encompassed details for each specific part of our area of study. If we failed any portion of the exam, we couldn't graduate on schedule with our class. During the 4th and final quarter of our 1st class year, during license prep, the transfer of 1st class officer responsibility for leadership of the Academy passed to the 2nd classmen. That allowed all 1st classmen to focus their complete concentration on passing the critical Coast Guard license exams. No pressure though!

We were issued all books and study materials in advance of the upcoming classes. Class schedules were fixed, and there were no electives at all until the 1st class year. The section we lived with at the company barracks was the same group we attended classes with, mustered for colors and meals with, ate with and spent our free time with. After our plebe year, we were forced to split up because of the "A&B Splits." When we returned for our 2nd class year, we stayed in our same section for the final 2 years.

During plebe year, we had to muster and march to class together. One plebe was assigned section leader duty for the week to get the section to class, take attendance, and give the muster report to the instructor.

There was never a delay. Everyone in the section knew the time that class started and the need to be seated and ready 5 minutes before the class began. When the instructor entered the room, everyone came to attention until the instructor told us to "take seats". The only acceptable reason for not being present in class was that you were in the hospital, on watch, or on a varsity team movement. Although it wasn't necessary for us to muster as upperclassmen, the rest of the procedures remained in place. We stood at attention when the instructor arrived right up to our final class. The muster sheet with details of all present or who was missing and why was signed off by the instructor. Our engineering class of 1971 was the last year to graduate with a slide rule and without a calculator. The group behind us, the class of 1972 had calculators available. The Bowmar pocket calculator came out in the fall of 1971 long after we graduated.

During our plebe year, we took the usual first-year engineering classes like advanced chemistry and calculus. We were also preparing for the following year that we would spend at sea. All of us took a course in emergency ship's medicine. There are no doctors in the middle of the ocean, and you better know the basics to care for yourself and shipmates should it be necessary for an emergency. As midshipmen training for engine room duties, we took classes in drafting, machine shop, pipe-fitting, and learned how to run lathes, milling machines, and surface grinders. We also had a training course in various welding techniques like arc welding, gas welding, and use of a blowtorch to steel cutting. This hands-on training was a blast and proved not only useful during our sea year but throughout our engineering lives.

Once classes began and the daily routine started to fall into place the pressure of being a plebe also fell into place. While it wasn't necessarily fun, it became clear that we had responsibilities and knew exactly how we were expected to perform. Plebes were the last group to receive a privilege in the regiment and the first to lose it.

One of the events that was especially fun and we had heard about from upperclassmen once our classes began – Firefighting! We made a trip to Bayonne, New Jersey to firefighting school for a day. We learned the proper use of fire hoses and various small refillable equipment for fighting smaller fires. We got to use oxygen masks and got inside of steel enclosure to put out a fire that was burning in a tank of kerosene. Ask any Kings Point graduate about firefighting school; they will give you a long story about what happened when they went. It's one of those things that's impossible to forget.

Plebe year was a gear up toward sea year. We also had to do a lot of paperwork during our sea year that was specific to the applications onboard the ship. The study material was called the "Sea Project" and once completed resulted in a stack of paperwork measuring 1 to 1.5 feet high. Our sea project was very structured and involved, and we received a grade for each section of the project. We had a schedule for completion and had to do a mailing on a quarterly basis to assure our instructors we were keeping up with our assignment schedule.

When football season was in full swing, there were things to prepare and anticipate. Homecoming was a lot of fun and an enormous event for the entire weekend. The 1st classmen responsible for organizing the details decided the plebes should build an ark – In actuality, it looked more like the side of a ship. Constructed with 2 x 4's and chicken wire there were plastic strips of black and white that spelled out "1967 WELCOME HOME KINGS POINTERS". Our entire class of plebes worked an untold number of hours on this crazy ark. Then, it fell over in a storm just days before homecoming, and we had to scramble to get it put back together and finished on schedule. We honestly had fun doing the work in preparation for the homecoming event. The last 24-hour rebuild made us feel a sense of accomplishment under the circumstances beyond our control.

The Homecoming Ark of 1967 that the plebes built under the direction of the class of 1968 event planners. A storm almost ruined our efforts.

The class of 1971 Plebes welcoming the team onto the field at Homecoming in 1967.

There are some formal dances specifically for 1st classmen leading up to graduation. Plebes often volunteered to serve refreshments and hors-d'oeuvres during some of the dances and parties. Once we learned how to follow and obey orders, it started to become an acceptable level of pain being a plebe. We also saw ourselves differently, and we were proud of our accomplishments as the fall progressed we looked forward to our very first leave since arriving in mid-July.

Each night, a Warrant Officer took over as the regimental overseer. His title was Regimental Officer of the Watch or ROOW - pronounced ROW-WOW. They wandered about the Academy grounds looking for wayward midshipmen that might be up to no good. They were the most feared duty officers by all of us all because no matter what you might be doing, if it happened to be wrong, a ROOW would catch you at it and you would be in seriously deep trouble. A good example would be on one of those mornings when you are truly dead to the world and didn't hear the bugle call for reveille. Perhaps you studied too late or were up to no good the night before, and you just don't move. There is a much better than even chance that you will get a knock on your door and a ROOW is waking you to let you know you are now on report for not being out of your rack after reveille sounded. How did he know when there are 750 other people in the regiment? They just did!

A big white mansion-style building named Wiley Hall is a centerpiece of the Academy and was previously the mansion of Walter P. Chrysler before the Academy site got started in 1942. Wiley Hall is the administrative headquarters for the Academy Staff Officers including the Superintendent, Assistant Superintendent, Dean, the Regimental Officer, Drill and Activities Officer, the Midshipmen Officer of the Day, and other Academy personnel. There were attractive "Officer Quarters" homes on the Academy grounds where the top eight officers resided. During our first few years at Kings Point, the Superintendent was Vice Admiral Gordon McLintock who was the Academy's 4th superintendent and had held that position since 1948. He and his wife lived in a beautiful house on the grounds of the Academy with a spectacular view overlooking the Long Island Sound. Wiley Hall was an unforgettable place and is an outstanding sight for anyone that passes by the Academy on a boat on the Long Island Sound.

Uniforms

When I remember all the uniforms we were issued during our plebe year and continued to wear for four years at the Academy, it amazes me. Most of them were utterly useless after we graduated. It's humorous that most people go through their college years wearing only a pair of jeans, a tee shirt, and sneakers.

Examining the uniforms by season, it's easy to understand that we needed detail instructions and assistance from upperclassmen to learn the proper way to wear them. Especially the formal uniforms which were unquestionably not intuitive. During events, there were always musters, and upperclassmen would inspect the plebes to make sure that each outfit got assembled correctly. During morning announcements, an essential piece of information was what uniform to wear that day. If there was a special event, like an honored guest for dinner, we might have to wear a different uniform than our daily working uniform for a special dinner occasion.

Summer Weather

Summer Uniforms: Long sleeve working khaki, formal dress C, short sleeve whites, dungarees with garrison cap, service dress white, service dress khaki, short sleeve working khaki.

Winter Weather

Winter Uniforms: Undress blues (CPO'S) with convoy coat, undress blues (CPO'S), service dress blue B, dungarees with watch cap, formal dress B, undress blues (CPO'S) with peacoat - peacoat was replaced by "A" jacket.

The space in our wardrobe lockers and overhead storage in our room was limited, and there was not enough room for all of these uniforms. Each deck in the barracks had a wardrobe storage locker for storing a footlocker or large suitcase to keep out of season uniforms. All midshipmen had strict uniform policies whenever leaving the barracks for any reason. Even the 1st classmen were subject to getting stuck for not wearing the proper uniform.

Study Hours

Study hours were Monday through Friday 1900 to 2200 – when Taps sounded. Before classes commenced, plebes had to have lights out at Taps. After classes started, plebes were required to have their lights out at 2300. Upperclassmen didn't need to turn off their lights – study continued well into the night. At 2150 before Taps, the tattoo bugle call was sounded over the regiment-wide PA system. Occasionally, we'd be in a group study setting, and it had to stop at tattoo. The library and other public buildings closed at 2200 and the only place we could be after Taps was in our own room. Tattoo was the signal to let us know we had 10 minutes to get back to the room. Nighttime rules got strictly enforced, and violators got suitable punishment.

Morning Colors and Daily Routine

At 0800 hours every morning except Sunday, no matter the weather, the entire regiment gathered around the oval in front of the administration building, Wiley Hall, to raise the remarkably large American flag on our 175 feet high flagpole. It is the tallest flagpole in the world without guy-wires. After the entire regiment assembled in their assigned positions around the oval, they stood at parade rest. The Midshipman Officer of the Day (MOD) stepped from the Wiley Hall portico and rang eight bells, then called the regiment to attention, and ordered hand salute while the regimental band played the Star-Spangled Banner.

Immediately following colors, we proceeded directly to our morning classes. We finished morning classes at 1130 and broke for lunch. Afternoon classes began at 1300 and concluded at 1600. From 1600 to 1800 was our only free time and for sports teams, it was practice time. The rest of us used it as a time for exercise and often that was at O'Hara Hall the gym building.

8 bells sound for Morning Colors outside of Wiley Hall Administration building

Retreat

At a specified time, each day near sunset, retreat took place. Retreat is the lowering of the colors and the time is preset on a schedule so that the color guard is in position for the ceremony. A retreat bugle call sounded by a recording over the regiment-wide PA system controlled by the office of the MOD in Wiley Hall. If you were anywhere outside and in uniform, you stopped and saluted during retreat. If you were not in uniform, you stood at attention. Naval service personnel never salute without a "cover" and never salute indoors.

Watches

Part of Academy life was standing watches. To those not familiar with the term watches, all military installations operate on a watch system divided into 4-hour increments. 4 hours on, 8 hours off. Related to Navy and Merchant ship watches, there is a team of people for the scheduled watch. On a merchant ship, there's a team on the bridge and a team in the engine room. The 3 watches are called the day watch, the morning watch, and the mid-watch. The day is 0800 to 1200 and 2000 to 2400. Morning is 0400 to 0800 and 1600 to 2000. Mid-watch is 1200 to 1600 and 0000 to 0400. The most attractive watch is the day watch and goes to the most senior people on the ship. 2nd is the morning watch and finally the mid-watch. The standard watch routine is to report early, 15 to 20 minutes, to become familiar with the log activities and anything abnormal that might be going on. Get prepared by getting a status review by the group on watch, discussion, and inspection and then when totally prepared, take over command of the watch and formally relieve the previous watch stander.

On a ship, the watch activities might be routine underway steaming at sea for days at a time as when crossing an ocean. But, it could also involve docking the ship or loading and unloading cargo. On a naval ship, it might include an exercise with live firing of weapons, underway replenishment or flight operations. The watch officer receives assistance during any significant activity by other officers on the ship who assume some responsibilities to ease the load of the watch commander.

The Academy watches were not nearly as critical, but they were equally as important to the functioning of the daily activities of the Academy. Security maintained and normal functions monitored and, if there is a problem, the midshipmen were trained to deal with the situation. It was all a part of the training process to prepare for life after school.

There were 4 categories of watches. Regimental, Battalion, Engineering, and Fire Watch. Each had specific times for standing the watch and duties to perform. Plebes were assigned to work with upperclassmen. They ran errands and learned the procedures and trained for the next level of watch standing when they became upperclassmen. Fire Watch got manned by deck midshipmen who focused on potential fires just as when onboard a ship. Engineering midshipmen stood watch in the Academy power plant that supplied steam for hot water, heating and washing facilities at the academy. All midshipman watches were manned 24 hours per day 7 days per week. Each company office got manned by midshipman watches, and some of those primary activities included receiving and sorting the mail and making company-wide announcements at various times of the day and evening over the company 1 MC.

We had an experience during our plebe year that demonstrated the importance of the watch system. Docked at Kings Point was a 12-meter sailing yacht named Weatherly that had won the America's Cup in 1962 and raced out of the New York Yacht Club. At the time, it was a very famous yacht because President and Mrs. Kennedy took particular interest in the America's Cup race that took place in Newport, Rhode Island because of their lifelong connection to that area of the New England coastline. Below 6th company in Jones Hall barracks, where I lived, was a sail locker on the zero deck that housed many of Weatherly's extremely large sails. A fire started in the sail locker one afternoon which could have burned down the entire company building. Due to the quick response of the Fire Watch team and the academy's onsite fire department, the fire was quickly isolated and contained to just the sail locker. There was very little damage, other than smoke to our building. A catastrophe was averted because of excellent training and the Academy watch system. It was never determined what caused the fire, but it was assumed to be caused by spontaneous combustion from some cleaning solutions inside the locker.

One Academy football coach was quoted as saying during an interview by a magazine reporter – "Players would tell me they wouldn't be at practice because they had firefighting school, or would be late because they had to stand watch in the boiler room. I thought they were putting me on!" He learned that the U.S. Merchant Marine Academy was an unusual college environment.

Liberty

Liberty was a privilege and not a right. As easily as it is given, it could be taken away.

Plebes

We were informed on our first day that our first leave would be on Thanksgiving and we would not be allowed to leave before then. However, on a couple of special occasions, we were given a chance to leave the Academy for a brief period. Homecoming weekend in October is one that comes to mind. We won the football game, and it was announced during the closing minutes that plebes would be given special liberty for 4 or 5 hours. Our company midshipman officers gave specific instructions, which uniform was required and we had to muster to get out and then muster again for a headcount when we returned. This was a very big deal at the time.

Once we were given our first leave for Thanksgiving, then a regular plebe liberty schedule went into effect. Because there were events held on Saturdays during nice weather like a parade review or football game, there were no fixed times for liberty on Saturday. The regiment was informed after the event was over who could go on liberty at what specific time. The upperclassmen departed on liberty first, and the last allowed to muster and depart, of course, the plebes.

Routine Weekend Liberty

1st Classmen

Liberty began after the event of the day on Saturday - Inspection, parade or football game. Muster was not required to depart once the time was established. 1st classmen simply "signed out" at the Vickery Gate guard shack. They were required to return by Sunday evening at 1900 (7 PM). Uniform required was either the dress uniform specified for the day or blue blazer with pocket crest, gray slacks, white shirt, and tie. Brown or black shoes including loafers were allowed. Dress overcoat or raincoat was optional.

2nd and 3rd Classmen

Liberty began an hour after the 1st classmen. The first group to depart had to muster, and after the first group you could check out at Vickery Gate. You were required to return Saturday by 2200 unless you had a preapproved overnight pass. Otherwise, you could depart at 0800 Sunday morning and be required to return by Sunday evening at 1800. Uniform required was either the dress uniform specified for the day or blue blazer with pocket crest, gray slacks, white shirt, and tie. Brown or black shoes including loafers were allowed. Dress overcoat or raincoat was optional.

Plebes

Liberty began an hour after 2nd and 3rd classmen. Musters were held, and inspection was required for all plebes before they left on liberty. Saturday return was 2000 for plebes. They could depart again Sunday morning at 0900 but had to be back at the Academy by 1700. Plebes were required to muster and have headcount immediately following liberty hours. If you were not present for muster after liberty ended, you were put on a list and might find yourself expelled.

Recognition Day

In late April, the regimental midshipmen officers reviewed the plebe class without our knowledge. Meetings were held with midshipman battalion and company commanders and the Academy staff officers including the Superintendent, Assistant Superintendent, and the Regimental Officer. The purpose of these review meetings was to determine if we met the qualifications to become 4th classmen. Naturally, we knew this day would come sooner or later, but there was no set schedule. It was determined that we were qualified and a day was established for our "Recognition Day." It's often referred to as the Run for Recognition.

The afternoon of our Run for Recognition, classes ended at mid-day, and we all gathered on Mallory Pier, the long main pier that, with Crown-inshield Pier and boat shed, formed Hague Basin. The run started by traversing a rope strung between the two piers about a 50-yard span. There were around 300 of us standing and waiting to start the rope traverse, but it wasn't long before we decided to take the plunge into the ice-cold water off the end of Mallory Pier and swim the 50-yard span to Crown-inshield Pier. After running the length of the pier and boat shed, we reached the warm water of the indoor Marshall Pool which helped return blood flow to our bodies again. The rest of the run was manned by upperclassmen with fire hoses and other forms of physical punishment, not too physical though. Then we finally reached the peak of the oval near the flagpole to salute the Regimental Commander and request his permission to become a 4th classman. It's a tradition that was always enjoyed by the entire regiment and one that was never forgotten. The bracing and square corners and other plebe requirements were finally over. We still had cleaning stations, but it was a small price to pay to feel like a normal human again.

Run for Recognition

For those who might think this service academy system is all crazy unnecessary nonsense, it honestly isn't at all. The purpose of going through plebe year is to train people to react under extreme pressure with prerequisite responses to take crucial action. It prepares your mind to think under pressure and not get flustered and forget the proper action required. For example, if an explosion took place aboard a ship, certain immediate actions are needed to avoid further destruction, and they must be performed without hesitation or delay. These are real-world requirements that would need to be learned and memorized for future application. The plebe knowledge and building names at Kings Point USMMA are still indelibly etched in mine and most other graduates' memories and can be recalled very clearly nearly 50 years later. Another valuable and memorable point as written in our plebe knowledge Bearings book by then Academy Superintendent, Admiral Gordon McLintock, was: "Obey all lawful commands, even when sometimes you resent them. Then when you rise to command, you know how the other fellow feels and how to give orders." He also advised us to always keep a sense of humor. Words well-spoken for sure!

Graduation for the Class of 1968

When June arrived, we experienced for the first time the graduation of a class from Kings Point, and this was special for us because it was the group that led us throughout our plebe year. We didn't attend the graduation ceremony and see them throw their caps in the air. We did, however, participate in all of the events that led up to graduation day and there were a ton of visitors and dignitaries around the Academy grounds for the week of events. Those of us left behind still had another month to finish our year. We had classes to finish and finals to take before we were done for the year. The barracks were busy during the remaining few weeks after the graduation events concluded. The 2nd classmen who were designated midshipman officers were taking over their responsibilities of running the everyday life of the regiment of midshipmen. They were also moving their rooms around for their upcoming final year as 1st classmen.

Our section 328 of 24 men had grown very tight, and we were all waiting to move forward to the next exciting phase of our education. We only lost 4 of our starting number during plebe year which was a minor miracle. I credit the friendship we all had and the commitment to each other to lose so few the first year. Most of us were going to start our sea year experience, and we had 8 plebes in our group that were taking sea year splits and would be coming back after a short break to start classes and play on fall sports teams. Meanwhile, with our increased freedom over a couple of months being 4th classmen and no longer plebes, we began to get to know some of our classmates that lived in other companies a lot better. It was much easier to make new friends once we were able to speak to other people outside of our rooms!

Some of our belonging had to be moved to storage until we returned from a year away from the Academy. Those included uniforms and other personal items that we didn't need until we came back. Then, we also had to pay close attention because before we knew it, finals were upon us. Everyone was antsy, and it was difficult to concentrate and stay focused. Some people got a little carried away, and there wasn't much that happened around the Academy that we all didn't know about within hours.

On the night before one of our finals, a few of our classmates decided it was time to pull a major prank. Late one night they drove a 2 ½ ton pickup truck into the outdoor swimming pool and deployed an inflatable life raft to sit next to it. The pranksters were never uncovered, but those of us in the know were aware. They went down in our class history as the first plebes to pull off a major prank without getting caught!

Chapter 3
3rd Class Sea Year

While I was growing up, my father remained active in the US Air Force Reserves and spent two weeks each year on active duty to maintain his position as a Major in the Air Force. As I write this, we are currently in the middle of a situation with North Korea which is escalating due to a loose cannon and crazy man, Kim Jong-un. He and his military are launching test missiles and threatening to continue nuclear weapons testing, and the attention of many Americans and others around the world are focused on North Korea. I state this fact because Kim Jong-un's father, Kim Jong-il, was the same type of madman and caused America to have a severe conflict that impacted my personal life during my years at Kings Point. The reason for the background narrative from the usspueblo.org website detailing the capture of an American warship will become clear as you continue to read this chapter about my sea year experience.

USS Pueblo Captured

Sasebo, Japan is a major U.S. Naval Base for the US Pacific Fleet and the primary facility for logistical support of forward-deployed units and operating forces in the Pacific theater. A look at a map of that area will show that it's the closest U.S. Naval base to the Korean Peninsula.

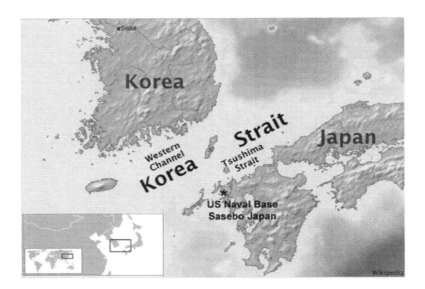

On January 11, 1968, an American electronic intelligence ship posing as an oceanographic survey ship named the USS Pueblo (AGER-2) departed Sasebo, Japan. They had stopped in Sasebo for a week to repair damage caused by very heavy storms in the Tsushima Strait between Korea and Japan during the previous week.

By Sunday, January 21, 1968, they were positioned off the coast of North Korea's port city of Wonsan, but due to weather and atmospheric conditions, they were not able to communicate with the Naval Intelligence Command Group in Japan. Meanwhile, on January 19th a group of 31 North Korean soldiers had slipped through the DMZ and crossed into South Korea and worked their way through the mountains to Seoul. By the 21st, they got behind the South Korean Army and penetrated to within 1000 yards of South Korean President Park's residence and office complex. They were finally discovered and attacked by South Korean soldiers and stopped before they could attack the complex. President Park and his ministers vowed to retaliate. Due to Naval bureaucracy and indecision, the admiral who was Commander Naval Forces Japan decided not to call Pueblo back from their spying position off the coast of North Korea. There was absolutely nothing on the television news reports in the U.S. about the confrontation at President Park's headquarters in Seoul and about a 1-inch comment in The New York Times that simply mentioned it as a "clash."

On January 23, 1968, Pueblo moved from its overnight position 25 miles from the North Korean coast to 15 miles off the island of Yo Do in North Korea, and they were dead in the water or intentional stopped and not making any "headway" with the two oceanographers aboard taking water samples with their test gear in the water and signal flags were raised so indicating. While Pueblo's Captain Bucher and his officers were eating their lunch in the wardroom, a call from the bridge informed the captain that a North Korean sub chaser was 8 miles out and headed toward Pueblo. Three minutes later another call came saying the chaser was now 5 miles out and approaching at 40 knots. The position of Pueblo was verified by radar to be 15.8 miles away from the nearest land while 12 miles or closer is considered North Korean sovereign territory. The sub chaser's men were at battle stations and at 1000 yards out, it asked Pueblo's nationality, and the captain responded by raising the US flag. An intercepted message from the lead North Korean sailor at 1210 to his superior on shore said *"The name of the target is AGER-2. I judge it to be a reconnaissance ship. It is American guys. It does not appear that there are weapons and it is a hydrographic mapping ship."* Three more torpedo boats were sighted coming towards Pueblo. The sub chaser moved to 500 yards and signaled with their flags - HEAVE TO OR I WILL FIRE.

Pueblo was still dead in the water, and Pueblo replied I AM IN INTERNATIONAL WATERS. Then 2 Mig 21s did a low flyover, and two more boats were sighted heading toward Pueblo. Pueblo got underway and started heading out to sea and even further away from land. A North Korean message intercepted at 1306 read *"...According to present instructions we will close down the radio, tie up the personnel, tow it and enter port at Wonsan. At present, we are on our way to boarding. We are coming in."* Pueblo increased their speed to 12 knots, and the men below decks on Pueblo were destroying all classified materials by shredding and burning and also destroying equipment with axes and hammers. The fast-moving sub chaser and torpedo boats began firing 57mm explosive rounds and machine guns. The captain and two other men on the flying bridge were wounded. Pueblo stopped, and the shooting by the North Koreans then stopped. The sub chaser signaled FOLLOW ME HAVE PILOT ON BOARD. Pueblo proceeded at 2/3 speed, then stopped. The firing resumed killing one crew member and wounding several more. Pueblo proceeded at 1/3 speed and continued destroying sensitive materials. They also stayed in continual contact with Naval Security Group in Japan by radio, so Naval Command was aware of the situation. The last message Pueblo received from Naval Security was "Some birds winging your way." The sub chaser commander signaled Pueblo to STOP. 16 miles from North Korean sovereign territory, 4 miles into International Waters, they were boarded. All of the men were tied up, blindfolded and gathered on the fantail. Any resistance was met with punches and kicks by the North Korean sailors.

Pueblo was docked in Wonson by a North Korean civilian pilot where the men were removed from the ship past North Korean civilians who were yelling and screaming insults at the Americans. Hispanic crew members were attacked by North Korean soldiers because they were thought to be South Koreans. The crew of Pueblo was then transported by bus and train to the first compound of their imprisonment.

> *** reference usspueblo.org for providing specific details of this incident. Go there to learn more about the facts surrounding the only time in over 150 years that a US flag ship has been hijacked on the high seas by a foreign military force.

Reserves Called to Active Duty

In the days following the capture of USS Pueblo by the North Koreans, President Lyndon Johnson called up fourteen Air National Guard, eight

Air Force Reserve and six Navy Reserve units. The Air Force Reserve active duty call-up of nearly 14,800 men included one Major Gustave Jockers, my dad. He got transferred from his regular reserve duty station at Stewart Air Force Base in Newburgh, New York to a Strategic Air Command base of B-52 bombers located in Blytheville, Arkansas. He remained there for a little over a year. I include this account in the Sea Year section of the account because of some unusual coincidences that occurred during my year at sea which will become clear. In January 1968, while I was in the 2nd half of my plebe year, my father began an adventure of his own.

Sea Year Begins

After the Class of 1968 graduated in early June, we had classes to finish, finals to take, and at the end of June our plebe year was finally over, and we were now 3rd classmen. For most of us, it was time to begin our adventure of a lifetime called Sea Year. We would be gone from the Academy for more than a year, but when we returned the following August, we would have matured by five years or more. During my sea year that started in late June of 1968 and ended in early June 1969, I spent over 325 days onboard six very different types of ships. During my travels, I visited Belgium, Sweden, Denmark, The Netherlands, Venezuela, Panama City, Japan, South Vietnam, Ecuador, Haiti, Jamaica, England, Scotland, Germany, and France. I didn't keep track of the miles, but I wish I could have the distance in frequent flyer miles today.

Kings Point had a port training officer located in each of the three major shipping ports of New York, New Orleans, and Los Angeles. They assigned us to ships for our sea year and arranged with the shipping companies to sign us onboard the ship. I shipped out of the port of New York. My first ship assignment was a container ship owned by Moore-McCormack Lines named SS Mormaclynx. It traveled between New York and Northern Europe. I made the transatlantic trip four times. The second vessel was a Sunoco tanker named SS Pennsylvania Sun that moved crude oil from Lake Maracaibo, Venezuela to Philadelphia where it was unloaded at a refinery. I made that trip three times. While it would be fun to go into detail on each ship and each trip, I will only tell the story about my third ship which is by far the most interesting. I was onboard a vintage World War II Victory ship that was taken out of one of the moth-ball fleets where it stood anchored since the late 1940s. We sailed from Savannah, Georgia to Da Nang, South Vietnam where I arrived on New Year's Day 1969 at the height of the Vietnam war.

Most people have heard or seen the mothball reserve fleets stored in various places around the country. Some fleets are on the Hudson River, some in rivers that feed into the Chesapeake Bay and another on the west coast in the San Francisco area. There are many spots where they remain at anchor rusting and rotting. During Vietnam, the supply of munitions and equipment for the war effort was performed by the MSTS Military Sea Transportation Service which eventually became the Military Sealift Command - MSC. MSTS took about 100 Victory ships out of the National Defense Reserve Fleet (mothball fleet), cleaned them up, got them run-ning and used them to transport goods. Da Nang was the home of the Marine Amphibious Force Logistic Command and handled the gear needed to support 81,000 Marines in Vietnam. In 1969, the total troops in South Vietnam exceeded 500,000.

The Military Sea Transportation Service had the job of bringing war supplies to Vietnam – 10,000 miles from the Pacific Coast. MSTS had four separate customers to serve: The Army, Air Force, Navy and Marine Corps. MSTS ships were staffed by "civilian" crews but carried 95% of the supplies used by our Armed Forces in Vietnam including airplanes, tanks, food, bombs, and ammunition into combat zones under fire. Crew mem-bers were given Navy grades and rank identification in the event of en-emy capture.

The 100 Victory ships that MSTS resurrected from the mothball fleet were assigned to private companies. The Victory ship I was aboard was operated by US Lines, and the Victory ships primarily carried ammunition and bombs. By the late 1960s, MSTS had 300 freighters and tankers sup-plying Vietnam, and there were 75 ships and over 3,000 merchant mari-ners in Vietnamese ports at any given time during this period.

USMMA had the unique and unenviable distinction during Vietnam as the only US service academy to allow their midshipmen to enter a combat war zone. In recognition of this service, there was a substantial number of midshipmen at Kings Point who were proud to wear the bar we were awarded for our service.

None of the four other service academies have permitted their students (Cadets or Midshipmen) to be exposed to the risk related to combat war zone active duty. We wore our service bar proudly.

Story of the Kings Point Battle Standard

The U.S. Merchant Marine Academy is privileged among the nation's five federal academies to be the only institution authorized to carry a battle standard as part of its color guard. The proud and colorful battle standard perpetuates the memory of the 142 Academy cadet/midshipmen who were casualties of World War II.

During times of war, members of the Army, Navy, Air Force, and Coast Guard engage in combat, but the students at their respective service academies do not. However, the students of the USMMA receive an integral part of their training at sea, and in the Second World War often found their lives in peril as they sailed through enemy-controlled waters or unloaded precious cargo in overseas combat areas. In all, 142 such cadet/midshipmen never returned to home port.

Just as in WWII and Korea, the men who ran these chartered ships for the Vietnam War were subject to the Uniform Code of Military Justice. In December 1966, the military was granted authority to take disciplinary action against the men on the ships that transported the goods for the war effort. During the period from 1964 to 1972, there were 138 instances of enemy action against the MSTS ships resulting in 16 merchant mariner deaths and 45 wounded.

The mothball fleet in the James River near Norfolk, Virginia. Santa Clara Victory was my home for three months as we crossed the Pacific to deliver our cargo of munitions in the harbor of Da Nang, South Vietnam.

I was assigned to the SS Santa Clara Victory that was built in 1945 and saw action in the North Atlantic until WWII ended and then it was mothballed. She was out of mothballs for a few years for Vietnam, and I got to take a ride on her for a few months. I believe it was returned to the mothball fleet in Suisun Bay near San Francisco. In mid-November 1968, I flew to Savannah, Georgia and then took a taxi far out into the Army munitions base where there were docks used for loading various weaponry onto ships tied to the piers. It was all new to me, and I arrived at night, so I didn't completely grasp where we were. I only knew that we were a long way from anywhere. Once I got aboard and reported to the Chief Engineer, I started to comprehend how old this ship really was. I was the only midshipman onboard, so I had a cabin to myself in the officer's area. I loaded my sea bag and suitcase into my room and wandered around the ship to meet a few more people aboard this relic.

The next day I had an opportunity to see that we were loading bombs and ammunition into the holds and were scheduled to get underway within the next couple of days. My new boss was the 1st assistant engineer, and he told me just to wander around and get to know the ship and introduce myself to people until we got underway and then he would figure out what he wanted me to do.

Putting the Trip Into Perspective

In 1969, cell phones, portable computers, and complex low-cost integrated circuits had either not been invented or had not made it into consumer's hands yet. We were onboard a vintage 1945 Victory ship that was a lot closer to a Ford Model T than a 1965 built ship which, by comparison, would be a Porsche 911 Turbo. I'll make a rough analogy to the trip I was on. I'll present you with a 1990 Toyota Tercel Hatchback with a 4-speed manual transmission and no air conditioning with 50,000 miles on the odometer. Drive it from New York City to Los Angeles and then back to New York, but make that cross-country trip seven times. Only drive 8 hours per day 7 days a week, and you cannot exceed 50 MPH. You can just use the tools that were available in 1990 when the Tercel was built. That means no cell phone and no internet access with a notebook computer. You'll be given paper maps and a compass. If you'd like to have a sextant for navigation, I'll gladly throw that in as well. Oh, the Tercel only has an AM radio, sorry. You can already begin to feel the pain. Just to ease a little of the burden for your trip, you don't have to carry any bombs with you!

The Trip West

The first leg of the trip was from Savannah, Georgia to Japan and we departed November 24, 1968. The Panama Canal leads to the Pacific Ocean, and this was my first trip through the canal, an engineering masterpiece. I was told that we would probably return to Savannah sometime in February. It was a surprise because I was accustomed to crossing the Atlantic in 5 days. It impressed me with the difference in the vastness of the Pacific. Then again, the other ships I was on were built in the 1960s and not in 1940s.

Before we departed, the old Victory ship was "cold." That means there were no fires in the boilers and our electric power for all onboard systems like lighting and refrigeration was coming from a power supply on the dock. Everyone worked during the day, and only minimal engine systems required monitoring by the engineers. It was my first opportunity to see a ship that was cold, and a lot of work was being done inside the boilers to get the old systems ready to keep working for the next few months. It was fascinating to climb inside the boilers to see first-hand what I'd previously only seen in drawings and photos. Previous ships I'd been on were never really stopped. All engine room systems kept running for the brief period when the cargo was exchanged. Container ships and tankers stayed at the dock for a day or two before getting underway again. I'm referring to merchant ships I was on in the late 1960s. Today, even the super-size container ships with more than double the capacity, the turnaround is 2 or 3 days in the US and as short as ½ day in Hong Kong. Though some maintenance can be performed while underway or in port, most bigger jobs get scheduled for dry dock or when the ship is entirely out of service.

Starting from cold to ready to get underway took a while – maybe 6 or 8 hours. We got the boilers buttoned up, lit them off and slowly heated up. The process is very complicated, and I will not go into those details for fear of causing those still awake to nod off. Plus, I forgot that procedure long ago. Once we were self-sufficient, we pulled the plug from the dock, and off we headed down the Savannah River toward the Atlantic. The Panama Canal is almost due south of where we started, but Cuba is in the way requiring a slight jog around that island obstacle.

The Canal met my expectations and then some. It's a marvelous engineering feat, and everyone should experience it at least once. Starting at Atlantic sea level, you take multiple locks up and get to Lake Gatun that is well above sea level. Then, cross the lake and take a series of locks down to the Pacific Ocean. I make it sound like it takes 15 or 20 minutes, but it takes more like 8 to 10 hours. If there are delays, you might have to wait for up to a day before you get started crossing the canal.

During our transit, we had a calamity on board. Some ships allow drinking on board. Some allow only beer and some frown on any drinking at all. The Santa Clara Victory was under MSTS and not a shipping company's control, and it was a non-drinking ship, and that was clear to everyone onboard. However, some sailors, especially the most seasoned, disregarded the rules. The chief boson's mate was one that didn't listen. After we made our passage through the Panama Canal, he started consuming any liquor he could find onboard. When he couldn't locate anymore, he started drinking everything else. He walked into my room at one point and said – "hey, what have you got to drink?" I told him I didn't have anything. He opened my medicine cabinet, found a fresh bottle of Listerine and chugged it down in a single gulp! In the next day or two, he had lost all senses. Our Chief Mate put a deck crew together to restrain him. The Captain decided to contact the US Coast Guard in San Diego to have them meet us with a cutter to take the chief boson off and let others deal with him. A funny experience, but I'm glad it was once in a lifetime.

I was assigned to work through a rotation of watches in the engine room spending one week at a time with each of the engineers. Then, I would do "day work" with the electrician and start the rotation over again. Onboard in engineering were 4 engineers. The Chief, 1st Assistant, 2nd Assistant and 3rd Assistant. On ships, while we all know each other's name, everyone is called by their position. Chief, 1st, 2nd, and 3rd. Chiefs don't stand watches. On this relatively small ship, there was nothing unique to do with the cargo we were carrying, so we had the minimal personnel. The watch engineers were the 1st, 2nd and 3rd. Also present in the engine room are an oiler and a fireman. Firemen are responsible for the boilers that make steam for propulsion and other equipment that operate by steam like the electric generators. Oilers take care of all of the remaining machinery in the engine room space.

On this classic old Victory ship, we had 27 people including one who didn't make it past San Diego, so we were down to 26. The entire complement was a Captain and Chief Engineer, two cooks – one for the wardroom and one for the crewmen. For the engine room, there were 3 engineers, 3 oilers and 3 firemen (3 watch teams). For the bridge and shipboard operation, there was a Chief Mate, 3 mates standing watch, 3 wheelmen and 3 bosons mates (3 watch teams). Also, we had a ship's electrician, a radioman and one midshipman junior officer (me). The trip going west across the Pacific Ocean was relatively uneventful and seemed to go quickly. I stood watches at various times rotating through the 3 different watch groups and then I did day work with the electrician for a week. Before long, we arrived in Sasebo, Japan on December 21, 1968, just in time to spend Christmas.

Midshipmen on a ship received a pay of around $250 per month. Since we were carrying dangerous material, everyone onboard was paid a 10% bonus. Then, we were going to a war zone, and any time spent in the region, we got paid double. We were in Japan in 1968, then the capital of "high-tech" electronic bargains and I planned to buy myself a reel-to-reel tape deck for Christmas. I got to know one of my shipmates that stood watch as a fireman in the engine room. He was a Vietnam vet who had been shot in the foot but recovered just fine, and his name was Dudley – easy name to remember. Like me, he was a photography enthusiast, and he also knew a ton about hi-fi equipment. His goal was to buy himself a top of the line Sansui amplifier. This voyage was his first time on a ship since he received his sailing papers to be a fireman.

Christmas in Sasebo, Japan

I had learned a little about Sasebo and knew that it was a big Naval Base for Logistics. I have since learned that it is also in the prefecture (like a state only in Japan) of Nagasaki. The city that received the 2nd atomic bomb ever dropped was Nagasaki. Nagasaki was only about 60 miles away. Our reason for going to Sasebo was to get staged by Naval Logistics to head for Da Nang, in the proper ship sequence. We were a little ahead of schedule, and we quickly learned that we wouldn't depart until the 26th, so that was an excellent opportunity for us to spend Christmas in port.

Here's the first of the eerie coincidences. The reason that my father was on active duty in Arkansas was that a ship was high-jacked by North Korea and the crew was still being held in a prison. The port we were now in, Sasebo, Japan, was the port that USS Pueblo departed from when it started its mission on January 11, earlier this year. We had been at sea for a month, and there was no way to get news about world events until we made port at the American Naval Base in Japan. Then, we could get news on the TV in the wardroom from the Armed Forces Network. Yes, the Pueblo was still being held, but the negotiations appeared to be making positive headway.

Now, here's the second uncanny coincidence. Two days after we arrived on December 23, 1968, the imprisoned officers and crew of the USS Pueblo were released from captivity. Of course, we heard a lot about this historical event because of our specific location in Sasebo. Many of the officers and friends of mine from the crew knew the circumstances about my father and I didn't need to pay for any of the beers I consumed that night. The following day Dudley and I went out and purchased our Christmas presents. I was able to reach my mother by phone from the Naval Base and celebrate with her from afar. We knew that shortly my dad would be able to return to his regular life. It was a beautiful Christmas present for all in my family and indeed the crew and family of the Pueblo. Americans forgot this event a long time ago, assuming they knew about it when it occurred. As a direct result of the year he spent on active duty in Arkansas, my dad was promoted by the Air Force to Lt. Colonel. It was a proud moment for our family and more cause for celebration when we were together again.

Today, USS Pueblo (AGER-2) is in Pyongyang, North Korea and has been on display there since 2012. It's a proud symbol for the North Koreans to demonstrate their strength and military superiority over the United States. Today, nearly 50 years later, nothing has changed with North Korea and the darkness of the vacuum where they exist.

The day after Christmas in 1968, we got underway in the morning and proceeded southwest 1800 miles to Da Nang, South Vietnam with our load of bombs and bullets. A twist of fate after the North Korean situation, while we were in Sasebo, we picked up 10 South Korean freight handlers who specialized in handling munitions and would offload our cargo in Da Nang. In 1968, 50,000 South Korean soldiers were posted in South Vietnam. We also brought two Marines with a full cache of weapons including hand grenades. The thing that was on our minds and not spoken about by any of us was the 1968 Tet Offensive. One year before, one of the most massive campaigns by the North Vietnamese and Viet Cong was mounted against the US and their allies. Tet is the Vietnamese Lunar New Year celebration, and in 1969 it would be in mid-February. As it turned out, Saigon and Da Nang were primary targets in February 1969, but we were already safely back in the USA by then! The Korean freight handlers we took onboard were happy-go-lucky guys who lived on the fantail of the ship. The fantail, located at the very back of the ship, is directly above the propeller. The noise and vibration are extreme, but not to these hearty men. They cooked their food on charcoal stoves, rigged a toilet with a seat out over the water for nature calls and slept on cardboard beds. The Marines were brought into the fold of the crew's quarters and lived among us.

Arriving in Da Nang, South Vietnam

As we approached the harbor in the early morning on New Year's Day 1969, it was Wednesday, but it felt like a Sunday. Everything was quiet and peaceful. We were moving slowly, and it was very still and calm. It was quite beautiful with lush green mountains sloped down to the ocean and small islands scattered about the entrance to the harbor. There were guys in small canoes fishing with nets. I remember thinking this seemed much more like arriving at sunrise in the Caribbean and it certainly didn't feel like we were in a war zone. The buildings had a French look about them, kind of like the building style in New Orleans. We dropped anchor out in the harbor bay area, and there were a lot of ships at anchor while only a few were tied up at the docks. With our cargo, we weren't allowed to dock. Nothing much happened New Year's Day as all of the Americans and workers were off for the holiday.

As the sun began to set, the two Marines we had onboard came out on the deck. I had gotten to know one of them over the past week, and I asked what was up? He just said, 'watch and you'll see.' The two of them took a position on either side of the ship. One was on the port side way up at the bow and the other on the starboard side back on the stern. They were watching the water over the side of the ship and slowly walked as that one headed to the rear and the other toward the front. They were always looking over the side into the water. After they switched positions front and rear, they both pulled pins on grenades and dropped them in the water. They continued this all-night long. About every 5 minutes there was another explosion in the water. Okay, I just had to understand what this was going on. I asked the Marine I knew – what's the story? Your ship is loaded with bombs and other explosives. The Vietcong want to sneak out in a small boat or swim out and attach an explosive to the side of the ship and blow it up. We're trying to prevent that from happening. I GOT IT!

My new friend the Marine guard that protected the ship from "swimmers" and our Sunday morning arrival into Da Nang, South Vietnam.

The following day a group of barges was pulled alongside our ship and tied up. The South Korean longshoremen operating the cranes and rigging we had on board began the process of unloading our cargo. They went non-stop all day long. While at times the loads looked a little precarious, everything went very smooth. My new found Marine friend told me that the battleship USS New Jersey was operating in the area and expected to be shelling that night. I had learned about battleships during my plebe year, but I never saw one and never thought I'd see or hear one in operation. While I couldn't see it that night, I definitely heard it, and I'm not sure I got any sleep. It was an unbelievable sound and feeling. The battleship wasn't anywhere near us, and I couldn't see it, but when it fired its 16-inch guns, it looked like lightning in the sky. First, you could feel a concussion in your body and shortly after hear the unbelievable sound. The sound of thunder doesn't quite do it justice. USS New Jersey was in Vietnam for all of 1968 and the first quarter of 1969. Its mission was to fire on targeted large installations or storage facilities and to collapse the tunnel systems used by the Vietcong soldiers.

Barges pulled alongside so the South Korean longshoremen could unload our valuable cargo of ordnance for the soldiers on the ground.

A Day Ashore in Da Nang

My Uncle Skip was in the Navy's Seabees and was stationed in Da Nang at the same time I was there. I didn't know exactly where he was located, so I talked with my onboard Marine friend and asked if there was some way I might track him down. He explained it would probably be pretty easy. There was a Navy Headquarters building called the White Elephant right in the dock area, and they would have records of all military personnel in the Da Nang area, and the Seabees would be pretty easy to locate. He said to take a launch to the docks, go to the White Elephant and start asking around. You'll be surprised how helpful everyone will be to get a visitor in touch with a relative. I asked the Ship's Captain for permission, and he thought it was a terrific idea. He wished me luck, and I worked with the Chief Mate who was in radio contact with the dockside people to coordinate the barge traffic. He arranged to have a launch come pick me up at the ship and take me to the dock. At the White Elephant, there were a ton of soldiers willing to help me. I explained what I was trying to do, and right away they said – "you're on one of those old Victory ships dropping off ammo, and your uncle's here somewhere – let's go find him!" They did a little research and said the Seabees are all out at Red Beach. Let's take a ride out and see if we can find him. Off we go in a jeep – it felt remarkably strange. I was dressed in a pair of jeans and a chambray shirt, riding in a jeep with some young lieutenant and we're driving through bombed out buildings and cratered fields by the runway to see if I could find my Uncle Skip. We got to the exact right place. My uncle's name is John Ahlers, but everyone called him Skip or Skipper. We found his commanding officer, and he was sorry to tell me they were out in the countryside for a few days building something and they wouldn't be back before we left. I gave him a note to give my Uncle Skip to let him know I made it there, and I'd catch up with him when we both got home. What an experience I had that day.

Telling my "war story" about my trip to find my Uncle Skip in Da Nang to Dudley and "Juice" while the Korean longshoremen enjoyed their dinner.

Heading for Home

In less than three days our holds were empty. We left the South Korean longshoremen in Da Nang along with our Marine escorts. Then we weighed anchor and headed east for home. I knew we had another lengthy period at sea, but at least we were headed back. I remember thinking, thank God I only had to spend a few days – think of the poor SOBs that are here for a year or more.

Our return trip took over 30 days to reach the Panama Canal. There was a delay because we ran headlong into a typhoon which was a terrifying experience. I had been at the edge of a hurricane in the fall on an oil tanker in the Gulf of Mexico, but the tanker was 750 feet long and filled with oil. Our Victory ship was only 450 feet long, we were empty and riding very high in the water. The concern with ships as old as the Santa Clara Victory is metal fatigue and the potential for a hull fracture. Today's addition of all kinds of weather and communication satellites to aid in navigation has changed the maritime world immeasurably. But, remember at all times, it can be extremely dangerous on the high seas during severe weather both then and now. I cringe each time I hear a weather forecaster say the words: "The hurricane is not going to hit land, and it will move safely out to sea."

We were in extreme weather for several days, and it was so rough that the only way to get a little sleep without falling out of our bunk was to jam a life preserver under the mattress and wedge your body between the raised mattress and the wall. Everything on a ship in very rough seas is subject to damage and has to be secured. Even doing this, many things were broken or damaged, and it took us a couple of weeks to recover. We made it through, and I was never so glad to see land as when we approached the Panama Canal in early February. I remember that we docked back in Savannah on Lincoln's Birthday in 1969. As a small reward, the Kings Point training officer for the port of New York gave me a cherry assignment aboard a combination 100-passenger/freight ship named Santa Magdalena owned by Grace Lines. It sailed between New York and South America carrying bananas and lobster.

Death of a Ship

The final ship I was assigned to was the SS CV Sea Witch owned by American Export-Isbrandtsen Lines, and it was less than one-year-old when I reported aboard. Her service life was short-lived when in June 1973, while departing the container port in Staten Island, she collided with a fully loaded Esso tanker. They were near the Verrazano-Narrows

Bridge, and between the two ships, sixteen men perished in the flame-filled crash. Sea Witch was removed from service after the disaster and the Esso Brussels was rebuilt and put back into service. I'm positive that many Kings Pointers will remember the tragic events that took place in New York Harbor. This video from July 2016, was prepared by U.S.C.G. Training films, and it tells the story in amazing detail. youtu.be/fKM59Y6MX5s

My sea year came to an end in early June 1969, and I was then scheduled to be on summer leave until the 2nd week of August, so I had ten whole weeks of vacation before I had to return to the Academy to start my 2nd Class year. That's the most time I'd had off since the summer after my junior year of high school. I felt like I was goofing off.

Summer Vacation – 10 whole weeks

1969 the Summer of Peace and Music

My dad had been back home for about four months, and I first saw him briefly after I returned from my long trip on the Santa Clara Victory. Now we would have time to reunite and tell our long stories to each other and our family. My sister had just graduated from college, in late May and would start a teaching position in Poughkeepsie in the fall. She was the first in our sizable extended family to attend college, and it was an excellent opportunity for us all to be together and enjoy our accomplishments together.

At the top of our priority list for this summer vacation was to complete the roof on our little barn and get as much of the siding finished as possible. The roof trusses were all in place, but our barn was a skeleton and in dire need of some skin. Many of my friends were back from college for the summer, and I imposed on them to help us with the roof in exchange for all the food and beer they could eat and drink. The drinking age was 18 at that time, and we were all 20 now and well-seasoned in the art of drinking beer without getting carried away. Everyone had a blast on the days we worked to finish up the barn roof. We listened to loud music and shared our experiences over the past couple of years. By the time the roof got finished, we all developed a severe tan from the bright summer sun in upstate New York. To this day, we still refer to those crystal clear blue sky days as "Adirondack Days."

My best friend from high school, Danny Riggins, was studying to be a science teacher and, as a serious athlete, minored in physical education so he could coach as well. He lived in the small town of Wallkill where I went to high school, and his dad was the high school principal. Danny was the oldest of 11 children in this fun-loving Irish-Catholic family. Their large house was off the main street, and the big front porch became the prime hang out for our extensive group of friends. We'd show up in the early evening after dinner carrying a six-pack, sit on the porch and tell stories and laugh. At any given time, there could easily be 6 or 8 of us sitting on the porch with a cold one in our hand. Danny's dad, Big Pete Riggins, was a hoot and he'd occasionally join us for a beer and bust our chops just because he could.

The ongoing topic all summer long was the Woodstock Music & Art Fair that was planned for mid-August in Wallkill. It was a controversial subject in the small town of Wallkill and always a ton of speculation about what was going on. Occasionally guys with long hair on motorcycles would ride around town and try as we did, we never got them to join us for a beer on the porch to get the inside scoop about Woodstock. Posters were starting to show up with specific dates and the top name rock bands that would be at the festival. Everyone loved live music in the 60s, and this would surely be a big hit. The anticipated crowd was projected to be 50,000 people, and they already paid a deposit on a 300-acre site to hold the outdoor 3-day long festival. What a great idea and it would make our little town pretty famous later that summer.

The first group of posters that showed up during the summer announced the upcoming Woodstock Festival in Wallkill, NY

A lot of the older folks in town were entirely against the idea of holding this crazy music festival, and they were up in arms and vowed to fight it in any way possible. It was an excellent topic for ongoing discussions and made for an exciting summer. Early in July, the town board passed a ruling that a permit was mandatory for a gathering of more than 5,000 people. Then, on July 15th, the board denied the request for the outdoor concert expected to reach 50,000 people because the portable toilets needed would not meet town code. The event got squashed along with the fun that was planned for mid-August. I had already worked out all of the details for the first weekend after I returned to Kings Point. As a 2nd classman, I would be able to take long weekends once I was back in school and it was before football season started. I was disappointed to know that every major band of the day was scheduled to play at this event.

By the first week of August, I started to get my stuff together to return to Kings Point both physically and mentally. I knew it would be much better than plebe year, but after being on my personal schedule for the past year, I wasn't looking forward to the regimentation and confinement that I would have to go back to for the next two years. I would also have to get a much shorter haircut before I reported back to the Academy!

Two good things got wrapped up before I went back to Kings Point.

We finished the entire roof on our barn including a fresh coat of shingles. We got about three-quarters of the walls finished with siding, and it was starting to shape up admirably. The second positive thing was that the plans for Woodstock were finalized and it was going to be held at a dairy farm in White Lake. My mother and father owned a little one-room cabin in White Lake, and I laid the groundwork for a group of my friends from Kings Point to go there with me the weekend of the festival. It was only a 3-hour trip, and it would be an easy achievement between 1:00 on Saturday and get back on Sunday night before the end of liberty. For a complete chronology of the events leading up to the Woodstock Festival, the best movie to watch is *Taking Woodstock* directed by Ang Lee who also directed *Brokeback Mountain*, *Life of Pi* and *Crouching Tiger, Hidden Dragon* among his other famous films. As we approach the fiftieth anniversary of The Woodstock Festival, I'm sure there will be ample opportunities to revisit the events that are so famous even today.

Chapter 4
2nd Class Year

Arriving back at the Academy turned out to be a lot more fun than antic-ipated. It was great to see all of my old plebe friends that I'd missed the past year. We were scattered all over at new company locations, and I ended up getting assigned to 4th company. Not one of my plebe friends were in the same company, and I was allowed to choose a roommate for my 2nd class year. I had no desire to live for the next year with someone I didn't know. It was too risky, and I'd prefer to make my own choice. Now I was stuck. Since we had to report back earlier than the first class-men, we had a weekend to sort things out and decide what to do. I picked out a room, but I remained without a roommate during that first day.

A couple of my good friends from plebe year, John and Fetus, told me that one of their friends from the same city they lived in Long Beach, New York also got assigned to 4th company. They told me about this guy, Tom McCabe, who would be a perfect match for me. He found himself in the same spot with no one he knew in 4th company. Tom and I got together and immediately hit it off and made a quick and simple decision to live in the same room. As Tom and I agree, it was one of the best decisions we'd made up to that point in our relatively short lives. Tom and I are still to this day the closest of friends. They say you're lucky if you have one hand full of close friends. Tom is one of the fingers on my one hand of close friends.

We got ourselves moved in and organized. Meeting each other's friends began the process of meeting new people from our class that we hadn't known before. It took a little while to get used to being an upper-classman and, although it was initially fun to bust the balls of the fresh new meat called plebes, it turned out not to be a high priority in either of our lives. Tom and I are both big music fans and many of my friends from plebe year were also nuts about music. Once I told everyone that my parents owned a small cabin on White Lake, plans started to get made at once to go to the Woodstock Festival. We were trying to figure out if we would have a regimental parade that weekend which would mean a later start and all the options were reviewed and discussed at great length.

The following week, everyone got back including the 1st Classmen, and we all readied ourselves for classes to begin. It took us a little while just to get caught up on what we left behind the day we walked out over a year ago before we started our sea year. Soon I discovered I still had an excess of leftover demerits from plebe year and I would be restricted to the Academy for the following two weeks with no liberty. That meant there would be no Woodstock in our future.

When Thursday, August 14th - Woodstock day - arrived, we heard about the traffic on the New York State Thruway going upstate and about all of the problems. Friday, it was raining outside, and news abounded with stories about masses of people heading north towards White Lake. The New York State Thruway got closed for a period. It's the first time that restriction came with a tint of luck. We either wouldn't have gotten to White Lake for the music event or would not have been able to get back before the end of liberty, and we would all be in a shitload of trou-ble. Thanks, Gus, for being restricted and avoiding disaster! As all of the fabulous stories came out over the next several years about Woodstock, although we weren't there, my friends and I had a story of our own.

2nd Class Year was pretty much a blur. We studied nearly non-stop. Both Tom and I had similar problems. We didn't have the gift of natural intelligence. We had to work extremely hard for every grade we got, and our course load was very hard. Our 2nd and 3rd quarters peaked at 27 credit hours, and it seemed every night we were studying for an important exam the following day. Most of our study nights were well past 2300 (11:00). We had two significant side interests during the year. Our addiction was pinochle, and we had a group of friends that played a lot, and we held tournaments and smoked Swisher Sweet cigars while we played. There were times we would have 8 guys playing two games of double-deck pinochle, and it got so smoky in the room that the windows came down even though it was winter and freezing cold outside. At least we could breathe!

Pinochle, smoke cigars, and study = Our 2nd Class year in a nutshell.

A group of us decided to find a reason to waste time while appearing to be working on something. Some clubs and groups were getting away with a world of free outings and opportunities to get away from the daily grind. Our problem was that we couldn't stand associating the groups of people that were in the clubs. We needed to invent our own special club and only allow entry by those people we liked and wanted in our "private association." We held meetings to determine what our private organization might be like and debated about different ideas. Eventually, we decided to start a Drama Club – naturally, none of us knew anything about acting, but that shouldn't stop us. The one guy we liked that had some legitimate acting experience was Dave Miles, and he was unanimously elected to be President of the Drama Club. It took us several weeks of goofing off and conducted meetings to decide on the play – *Mister Roberts* - finally. It was an oldie but a goodie and fit perfectly with the theme, so we didn't even need to get too creative with costumes and set decoration.

It started as a world-class boondoggle and ended as a success both as a play and a way to have our own private boondoggle with the support of the administrative staff officers!

It was the ultimate boondoggle, but it turned out that we started to have some fun. We put on the play a couple of times and enlisted one of the local all-girls Catholic colleges in the area, Malloy College Drama Club, to help us through the process including things like makeup and decorations. One of our bonus feats was having the girls from Molloy, a local Catholic college for women, hang out with us during weekday nights without even breaking the rules. All in all, what started out to be a way just to goof off and eliminate some of the winter grind turned out to be a fun learning process for us all.

Tom was from Long Beach, and it was a very lucky thing for me. I got to know his mom, dad, and 2 younger brothers really well and would go to their home on Sundays for the most amazing dinners possible. His mom was of Italian descent and his father Irish, of course. Mrs. McCabe's objective was to make us no longer fit in our uniforms. Five or six-course meals were standard, and the food was just spectacular. She made a variety of foods my mother didn't cook, and the whole experience was the absolute best.

Until January 1985, the drinking age was 18, and that covered well over 90% of midshipmen. The main road out of the Academy is Steamboat Road. About a half-mile from Kings Point Vickery Gate was the upperclassmen hangout named Maurice's. Beer and food were overpriced, and it was wall-to-wall Kings Pointers drinking far too much and standing in line at the bar for their next beer. It was positively not my kind of place or the place that my buddies and I hung out. We had our private spot in Great Neck named The Club Tavern where the tap beer was inexpensive and cold. It was pretty small and had a few booth tables and a bar. They had no food service, but the owner didn't mind if you brought food into the bar. It just so happened that next door was an Italian sandwich shop that I still miss to this day. A 12-inch veal parmigiana hero was like $1.50. We told no one about our spot to keep it to ourselves. You could spend a Saturday afternoon at "The Club" for $2.50, and it was hands-down the best place for us. The only King Pointers present was our group of friends.

Our good friend Sully was a year older than most of us because he had to repeat his plebe year. Sully hailed from Jacksonville and had a long-time steady girlfriend that was studying to be a registered nurse. During our 2nd class year, Sully's girlfriend, Candy, moved from Jacksonville to work at North Shore Hospital in Great Neck and a 15-minute drive from Kings Point. Yes, it's the same hospital that Jennifer Lopez had her twins in and took over an entire maternity floor. Candy got an apartment within walking distance to the hospital, and it became our go-to place. She was like a mom-adviser to our whole group of friends, and she was an angel. Always willing to give us advice, especially about girls and troubles we had at the Academy. It was a perfect place to watch a Sunday football game and have a few beers before heading back for another tough week of classes and study.

As painful as our 2nd class year was, our entire group of friends had a good time on weekends. We also began to experiment with sneaking out after hours and going "over-the-wall" for a few brews. The choice night was Thursday night anticipating a little time off for the weekend and unable to wait any longer. We knew some midshipmen got caught at Maurice's after hours and O-T-W a.k.a. AWOL. That can be the end of an Academy career with the possibility of getting expelled. We had our resident OTW professional whose name was Kevin McParland. We all learned the safest way out and back in from our buddy Kev, and we had a hangout on Steamboat a little past Maurice's named Curry's. When we went to Curry's we were the only white men in this little hole in the wall bar, and it was just perfect. The regulars got to know and like us a lot and enjoyed our humor and thought it was funny that we snuck out of school and went to hang out at their local bar where the patrons were almost exclusively black. It got so that we only had to buy about half the beer we drank and it was ideal. None of the officers at school would ever look in Curry's bar to catch us doing the forbidden deed O-T-W, and it was a fun place with a great selection of music!

We created a little trouble during our 4 years and this plaque is a marker for Kevin's Gate

Over the 2nd and 1st class years, we got to be pretty good at going over the wall, but we were always just rookies compared to Kevin. He has a plaque that a group of his friends dedicated in his memory at the McParland Gate at the exact location we quietly exited and returned. RIP Kevin.

During our 1st class year, the first time my girlfriend, Nancy, picked me up on the unlit road that ran just beyond McParland Gate with her lights off, she incorrectly assumed it was only me all dressed in dark clothing and dropping down over a wooden fence. In minutes, her little blue Cougar was packed with about six extra riders who were headed down the street to Curry's for an hour of relaxation and arm bending. Eventually, Nancy got used to having additional people using Kevin's gate to join us on our mid-week evening dates.

Music

Live music was everywhere, and I was lucky to have a roommate who lived nearby. We spent many of our Saturday nights at the local bars, clubs and music venues in the Long Beach, Long Island area especially during nice weather when people were filling the hot spots to capacity. On one summer evening at a place called The Beach House, I saw a band perform named Vanilla Fudge. Though never as popular as the most prominent name bands, I liked their unique style of music. In a standing only venue with a low ceiling and overly crowded conditions, we lost our hearing and drank our fair share of brew while they played their "psychedelic symphonic rock" music to our delight!

The Fillmore in San Francisco is still alive and well, but for a few short years from mid-1968 until mid-1971, The Fillmore East was the home of some of the all-time greatest bands in the world. It was located on the Lower East Side, now called the East Village neighborhood in New York City. Groups performed that are still popular today including the Doors, Jefferson Airplane, Jimi Hendrix, Sly and the Family Stone, Grateful Dead, Beach Boys, Joe Cocker and the list is any band that was playing live music during the three years that Fillmore East existed.

Fillmore East - Open 1968 ~ 1971

A group of four of us went to see Felix Pappalardi, Leslie West and their band named Mountain perform. It was so good and oh so loud. It was pretty strange anytime a group of us went out to a live concert. It didn't matter how we dressed; everyone looked at us with puzzlement. During the height of the hippie generation, antiwar protests, and free love we were an anomaly. Everyone had long shaggy hair, and we had almost none at all. We wore the clothes and shoes that everyone else was wearing, but we just didn't quite fit in. As we took our seats in the upper deck mezzanine (cheapest we could get), people were swallowing their joints thinking that for sure we had to be narcs. After we were there for a little while they realized we were just a group of characters who attended some military school and all the joints quickly reappeared. For the next several days our ears were ringing, and now we understand why so many of our generation have a bit of a hearing problem!

Spending Money

Although we received pay during our sea year and a lot of it was banked for future use, soon our "funny money" was gone. While we didn't have to pay for our education, books, clothes, or even our haircuts, we still had miscellaneous personal expenses. My folks had me on a $20 per month allowance during my last two years which was plenty to keep me in cherry cokes and toasted rolls at the Academy canteen, but it didn't go far when you had a couple of dates or party times during a given month. A lot of us worked one or two days during liberty on weekends to earn some extra spending money. It was easy to get a job in the local communities around Kings Point and Great Neck doing odd jobs like raking leaves and cleaning gutters, but they only paid $1.00 or $1.25 an hour, and it was backbreaking. Since I learned to be a pretty good handyman during my childhood, I was able to capitalize on what I knew. I had a close friend who also knew his way around a hammer and saw, and we teamed up to be a KP Handyman team. We soon had enough jobs to build a resume and have references to keep our higher paying jobs coming. My friend, Jon, and I would fix leaky faucets and toilets and do small repair jobs and received a premium. I recall we once took a job at a young couple's first home to install a faux brick backsplash in their kitchen. It took us a couple of weekends working 6+ hours per day, and we received $2 an hour. They liked our work so much we even got a bonus. It sure beat raking leaves for ½ the rate!

Our class workload was a pressing burden the entire year. Tom and I were up late almost every night studying and preparing for, what seemed like, a daily exam on one subject or another. We didn't participate in enforcing the class system on the plebes that lived on our floor. Instead, we became their protectors and guides to doing things the right way and let the system work for them and not against them. We had a coffee maker (illegal appliance) in our room. We'd have one of our favored plebes in for a cup now and then. In return, it was their job to make sure we didn't back to sleep after reveille sounded in the morning. The punishment for getting caught was a serious offense and led to at least 1 week of restriction. The assigned plebe had to scramble to our room to be sure we were NOT in the rack. Instead, we would move our pillows and blanket to our chair and go back to sleep bent over at the desk with our head on a pillow. This was not against the rules and qualified as not being in the rack after reveille and allowed us to log an extra 30 to 45 minutes of much-needed sleep.

In the days before cell phones and the breakup of the Bell telephone monopoly, making a "long distance" phone call was expensive. The greater the distance, the more expensive the call and time was measured in 10-second increments. A local call might be within 25 miles and only cost 10 cents, but anything further could easily mount up to multiple dollars for a 15 or 20-minute phone call. Every floor had at least one phone booth with a door. The phones were all coin-operated old fashion designs that were connected to permanent wires below the wall mounted coin phone, and there was a small desk below the phone. One of the 1st classmen on our floor worked for a phone company during his summer break between 2nd and 1st class year. He became one of our buddies and would stop by for a cup of coffee once in a while.

Early into our 2nd class year, our 1st class buddy told us what he learned over the summer and we were sworn to secrecy and could only tell our most trusted friends. Under the desk in the phone booth was the wire connector junction box for the phone. In the phone booth, just down the hall that most of us used, the cover was loosened and easily removed. After removing the cover, he had cut and stripped the yellow wire, and it was twisted together to maintain the connection. When we wanted to make a call, we inserted a nickel into the phone and waited for a dial tone. Upon getting a dial tone, disconnect the yellow wire and make the direct dial long distance phone call. After the call was over, we had to wait to insert a bunch of coins to pay for the call. After depositing our coins, reconnect the yellow wires and back came our coins. The system was flawless, and we never paid for a long-distance call again for our remaining two years at the Academy.

When spring came that year, we all caught a severe dose of spring fever. Our brains were getting numb from the year-long workload, and we began to daydream about the upcoming 1st class year when we could start to see the finish line.   In early June, we watched the class of 1970 graduate, and our class took over the reins of midshipmen command of the Academy.   We took our final exams for the year and departed in late June to return in about six weeks to be the next in line to enjoy graduation year.

Chapter 5
1st Class Year

1st Class Year

We returned in mid-August with smiles on our faces as we were looking forward to our final year. I spent the last summer with my parents and enjoyed my vacation time. My good friend Tom spent his vacation, as always, being a lifeguard at Long Beach and we started our final year as roommates again. During our 2nd class year, we were in an enviable location on the 2nd deck in 4th company, and for our 1st class year, we moved to the 3rd deck with the same perfect room located at the end of a hallway. It was a great location, and our room was once again the hangout for most of our friends. We had to be the only room in the regiment with a park bench in our room! For whatever reason, we seemed to fly well enough under the radar at all times to get away with almost anything as long as we didn't make trouble and set off blips on the radar screen of the Academy officers who would then start watching us far too close.

One of the best fringe benefits of 1st class year is the privilege of having a car and keeping it in an assigned parking spot in a lot just outside Vickery Gate on Academy grounds near Roosevelts Field House. My mother had just gotten a new car during the summer, and she loaned me her old model 1963 Plymouth Satellite to use for the year. It had to be one of the best gifts I'd received to date and much appreciated. A friend of mine gave it a fresh coat of paint that began to peel about halfway through the year. But, it was personal transportation and weekend freedom! It was known in the nearby small towns that King Point graduates got exceptionally good-paying jobs after graduation. A number of the local car dealers would sell 1st classmen a car in January for no money down and no payments due until after graduation. The temptation was far too big for many to resist and they would join the number of predecessors who went into debt before they even had a job. However, there were definitely some good looking high-end cars in the 1st class parking lot come springtime each year.

On Labor Day weekend, Tom was restricted for a problem he had at the end of our 2nd Class year, and he was left standing watches and vegetating at the Academy for the entire long weekend. On Saturday night, a group of us decided to go to a hot bar spot named the Oak Beach Inn (OBI) just past Jones Beach. On this late summer night at the beginning of my final year at the Academy, I met my future bride to be, Nancy. As often the case, you get hit by lightning when you least expect it. I had tired of the effort we collectively wasted desperately seeking the favor of the opposite sex and decided I would focus my 1st class year on my studies and being a "clean-cut all-American Midshipman." We had a large group of guys for this outing, and we were driving several cars. The OBI was directly on the beach, and an excellent live band venue and everyone was drinking, dancing and enjoying themselves.

A few of us were attracted to a small group of girls sitting and talking. There was one in particular that I had my sites on and asked her to dance and offered to buy her a drink. She didn't have much to say and told me she just had a root canal that day and didn't want to be here and was forced by her friends. Of course, I assumed it was a joke and thought - yeah, right! So, I danced with one of her girlfriends and let her sit by herself recovering from her "root canal." We all had a good time, and I found out while talking to Nancy's girlfriend that she honestly did have a root canal done that very day. When we saw the girls to their car, and we prepared to depart, I asked Nancy for her phone number. When she gave it to me, I thought, well maybe I'll give her a call and check on her recovery status. Later in the week, I called, and we set up a date for the following weekend. When I showed up at her parent's front door dressed in a blue blazer, white shirt and tie and my very short hair, I thought her father was going to shake my hand off and that her mother might just kiss me. In 1970, it was pretty unusual to see a guy who looked and dressed like me picking up your precious 20-year-old daughter for a date. I learned much later that my father-in-law was a sergeant in WWII and a Normandy D-Day veteran and he was extremely happy when my wife got interested in a young man who was attending a Military Academy. Throughout my last year at school, her parents were exceptionally kind and helpful to me, and I could not have been more content.

I decided to get involved in a group that was working to form for the first time a representative organization for midshipmen to work with the Academy administration officers to bring about some changes in Academy regulations and policy. We settled on the name Midshipmen Council, and it was similar to student council government which I took an active role in during high school. Our first effort for this newly established entity was a big job. To institute a formal honor code system that included disciplinary repercussions for both the violator and also someone who knew of a violation, but didn't tell. Eventually, our Academy Honor Code got executed, and it was the first formal honor code that existed for USMMA. It was a difficult undertaking and very satisfying in the end as it justified the reality of the Midshipmen Council organization.

Our second accomplishment, which might have been an even more daunting task, was to implement a new system that allowed us to skip classes on a selective and controlled basis. For almost 30 years, midshipmen had only three reasons to skip a scheduled course instruction lesson: In the hospital, standing a watch or on a trip for a sports team. We wanted to have a way to skip class for no ground except personal reasons. Other colleges had a class-cut system in place, and our class schedules were far more difficult, and sometimes we needed a break. It just made sense. There was a universal desire of everyone at the Academy to find a way to initiate a system, and Midshipmen Council seemed like the perfect vehicle. We started our effort with a campaign to make this happen. We had gray tee shirts printed, and we sold them at cost to nearly everyone in the regiment to show our solidarity. It merely read in two lines in black print - WAR COLLEGE - NO CUTS. Before big scheduled games or similar special occasions to generate spirit in the Regiment, we'd hold events like crazy hat day or dress down day during evening mess. During one of these "raise the spirit" events we spread the word that everyone should wear their WAR COLLEGE tee shirts. It made a loud statement! After several months of working on a written plan, negotiating with the Dean, the Department Heads, and the Assistant Superintendent, we finally achieved our goal. We worked out an agreement that allowed us two class cuts per quarter for each class. This applied only to 1st, 2nd and 3rd classmen. It was an enormous success for the newly formed Midshipmen Council, and we were able to take advantage of the cut system during the 3rd and final quarter of our 1st class year. The name was changed to Midshipman Council the following year, but I believe the council continues to operate and it was a good tradition we founded during our 1st Class year.

midshipmen council

Seated: R. Harkins, J. Jockers, T. McShane, P. Barnhart, B. Stoeffel, R. Wilson, D. Uttenkoff
Standing: B. Gibbs, M. Shanks, J. Rodrigues, K. McFee, F. Williams, J. Hardy, J. Bultmeyer

During the year-long build-up to graduation, there are special events that were strictly for 1st classmen and, as we observed as underclassmen, they were exciting and smash hits for all attendees and their dates. For some events, per tradition, we'd have plebes serving, and it was fun and engaging for them as well. It also caused us to remember how much fun it was when we were the plebes doing the serving because of the boisterous nature of the event plus all the great looking girls. Some events were held at the Academy like the Ring Dance held in celebration of getting our graduation rings. Others like the 100 Nights Dance were held at a local venue like a hotel. 100 nights (more or less) before graduation, this party was the kickoff for various parties held celebrate graduation. I distinctly remember the night I picked up Nancy to go to the Christmas formal which was the first of many she attended during my final year. I arrived at her home to pick her up in full dress uniform. Her father couldn't take enough pictures, and I'm sure I've never seen Nancy's mother smile as hard as she did that night. It's pleasant to look back at this exciting and eventful time when our life together was first starting out.

Formals and fun led to the day we got to toss our hats!

Sometime during the first quarter of our 1971 graduation year, I realized I had fallen in love for the first and only time. I asked Nancy to go with me to my home to meet my parents, my sisters and other family members. During the trip, I gave her my class pin which was a replica of the side of my class ring. Engaged to be engaged is a pretty serious yet exciting time. During the visit, Nancy learned that everyone called me Jack instead of Gus and she quickly fell into the habit. She seemed to like Jack better than Gus. After we returned to Long Island and my newly pinned girlfriend went back to her college classes, she told her friends all about the trip and the big event of getting pinned to Jack. Jack this and Jack that until – 'wait, I thought you fell in love with Gus, and we all like him. Who's this guy, Jack?'

Ice Boating on the Hudson

Growing up in Orange Lake, New York, I spent a lot of time on the water. In the summer my favorite pastime was sailing. I liked the effort and thought required to use the wind to get from point A to point B. Sometimes it was necessary to first go to C, D and maybe E before you finally got to B. Unlike a motor driven boat, it took a little longer to get where you wanted to go, so it's best to enjoy the ride and not try to meet a schedule. When winter arrived, our form of entertainment on the water turned to iceboating. While just as challenging to go from A to B, the speed was a whole lot faster. The most exciting thing about iceboating was to learn how to lift one of the runners or skates in the air so that you are balanced on two runners instead of all three. This act is called hiking in iceboat terms. You better know how to operate sails to get back on all three runners to avoid the biggest fear which is tipping the iceboat over!

My favorite uncle was my mother's brother, my Uncle Bob. He was not just a funny and entertaining guy, but he became a friend of mine when I reached my mid-teens. He was a carpenter who specialized in finish trim work like door trim, baseboards, and cove molding. He taught me all of the tricks about how to do trim work properly, and we did the finish work for two or three houses together while I worked for him in the summer between my sophomore and junior years in high school. We had a blast while I learned a lot. Uncle Bob was also my iceboat teacher. He had a very old style classic iceboat called a stern steerer that looked like a classic old sailboat. The sails were gigantic, and it wasn't as fast as many of the iceboats, but it was a blast to ride on.

The Hudson River often froze in the northern parts, mostly north of West Point. Occasionally, we would load an iceboat onto a big trailer and take it to sail on the Hudson River. It was an unusual challenge because the center channel of the river didn't freeze. You needed to be sure not to go too far out otherwise you'd break through the ice. The iceboat would sink and be gone forever - not to mention the threat to your body in the water! The winter of 1971 was exceptionally cold, and the Hudson River froze much further south than it had in many many years. There were frozen areas of the river south of the Tappan Zee Bridge near Tarrytown, New York only 25 miles north of Manhattan! Sometime in February, my Uncle Bob got hold of me and said he wanted to take his big iceboat on a trailer down the Hudson near the Tappan Zee Bridge area and asked me to join him. I inquired if I could bring some friends and, of course, his response was "the more, the merrier!" Nancy and I invited our friends Sully and Candy to bundle up in our warmest possible clothes to head out for some iceboating on the Hudson near the Tappan Zee on a Sunday morning. We drove north from Kings Point and met Uncle Bob and loaded his big boat down the ramp at a marina and set sail. Nancy, Candy, and Sully had never even been near an iceboat, and now they were doing something very few iceboaters have ever done. The Hudson has tides, and there is a high percentage of salt water in the water that far south. The cove area we were boating was absolute perfection. There was practically no snow on the ice, and it was very smooth like an ice rink. We went iceboating for several hours until we couldn't stand the cold anymore and our faces were frozen and bright red. We put the Uncle Bob's boat back on his trailer and then walked up the hill and found a little pub. In that bar, my wife discovered a brandy Alexander that she still refers to as the best one she's ever had PERIOD! All four of us still remember that experience as one of the top 10 things we've probably done – lifetime!

While the formal dances and parties were great, there was always a dark cloud that loomed over us during our 1st class year. In May before graduation, we had to sit for our Coast Guard license exams. Failure meant that we wouldn't graduate with our classmates. All structured classes ended after we took finals in the 3rd quarter of our 1st class year. We would spend our final full quarter preparing to sit for our Coast Guard license. There were formal prep classes with senior instructors for each of the five subjects that comprised the exam.

An Obligation Change Targeting Engineers

About a week before license exams started, our entire class was summoned to Bowditch Auditorium for a meeting with the Academy "top brass," a representative from the Department of Commerce, and a captain from the Navy. The atmosphere had an ominous overtone, and everyone was tense. The obligation we all signed and swore an oath to during plebe year had options. We could go into the US Navy or Marines and spend a minimum of 3 years on active duty. We could find a position with an American shipping company and sail on a U.S. flag merchant ship for 8 months per year for 3 consecutive years or 6 months per year for 4 consecutive years. Sailing on a US Flag merchant ship meant that, in most cases, we had to be a member of the union. For those of us who studied engineering, it was the M.E.B.A. union – Marine Engineers' Beneficial Association. Those graduates who studied nautical science, and trained to be a deck officer, would need to join the N.M.U. – National Maritime Union. US Flag company owned oil tankers were non-union positions, coveted, and highly sought. Jobs on non-US flag merchant ships, Panama and Liberia flags were prevalent at the time; the pay was a fraction of the union positions.

We were gathered to hear a critical announcement that there would be a change in the obligation for the class of 1971 and to our graduation class only. The circumstances that year were unique, and adjustments would need to be made. The MEBA union had announced that it was closing its books to US Merchant Marine Academy graduates and we would be blackballed from joining the union until further notice. After years of building up the effort to support the war in Vietnam, the US Navy found itself with an overabundance of Ensigns graduating from NROTC in colleges throughout the country, State Maritime Academies, and OCS

(Officers Candidate School). The number of billets available to Ensigns in the Navy and Second Lieutenants in the Marines was notably limited. We were, therefore, informed that there wasn't room for us and they decided for our graduating class the U.S. Federal Government was going to add another option to allow us to fulfill our obligation to the United States in return for our free service academy education.

Upon graduation, we would still be commissioned in the US Naval Reserves as Ensigns. The newest one-time option was to perform ACDUTRA (Active Duty for Training) for 30 consecutive days within each anniversary year after graduation for three consecutive years. Then we had to remain in the Inactive Reserves for 8 additional years for a total of 11 years' reserve status after graduation.

MEBA Conflict of Interest

A man named of Jesse M. Calhoon held the position of Union President of M.E.B.A. from 1963 to 1984. In the mid-1960s, Calhoon was approached by the federal government and maritime industry leaders to help find a way to meet the critical shortage of qualified marine engineers needed during the Vietnam War. Calhoon started Operation LEAP (Licensed Engineers Apprentice Program) and set up a training school at an old hotel in Baltimore named the Southern Hotel and named the union school the Calhoon MEBA Engineering School in 1966. In October 1968, Calhoon MEBA school graduated their first class after 2 years training which included 6 months spent aboard merchant ships at sea. The 19 newly graduated men were presented with great fanfare to the press and Calhoon declared that the best inducement for attending the program was that it was not only free to attend, but the "cadet" received $200 pay per month while training. Calhoon's "cadet engineers" got an open ticket to the MEBA union which became an exclusive club for MEBA School graduates only. Calhoon and the MEBA union built a dues base from within and eventually lined their coffers with their homebuilt membership dues paid for by the shipping companies.

The Calhoon MEBA Engineering School graduates were not commissioned officers in the US Navy and did not have a BS Degree in Engineering. They were simply graduates of a trade school that prepared them to pass a Coast Guard exam. The graduates were also the recipients of membership in the MEBA union and the high paying positions on American merchant vessels for their members. Three years later in 1971, Calhoon and his namesake "Engineering School" had built up sufficiently to support the proclaimed "needs of the federal government and maritime industry." He was putting out enough graduates to staff the engine rooms of the ships needed to supply materials for the Vietnam War. He then decided to close the union books to USMMA engineers whose four-year engineering degrees were paid for by tax payers and who had an obligation to the United States in return for their education.

This very same MEBA union in 1988, after Calhoon retired and C.E. DeFries succeeded him, was investigated and found guilty of conspiracy, embezzlement, extortion and mail fraud under the RICO. The Racketeer Influenced and Corrupt Organizations Act of 1970 went after bad guys, and MEBE holds the distinction for being the very first governing body of a union to be successfully prosecuted under the RICO act. DeFries and 18 of his crooked cronies went to jail. Poetic justice was served, and I'm most gratified to know that I was never obligated to pay a penny to that corrupt union.

I have to admit; It didn't take many of us long to decide to serve 90 days on active duty in the Navy over the next 3 years. It made the license exam we were about to take much more about graduating together with our class than it did about holding a license in my hand as a 3rd Assistant Engineer in steam and diesel power plants.

There were 5 days of tests and each day had a different area of focus. The test event took place on the main floor of the gym, O'Hara Hall, with 200+ midshipmen taking the test at once. In the final two weeks, before exams started, it seemed like there was no sleep by 1st classmen and we walked around like zombies. Finally, the day arrived and luckily the first day was math. It was much more fundamental and application-oriented than the college level advanced math we learned in our Academy classes. It was a "warm-up" breeze to get us started. Tests started at 0800 and stopped at 1200 for a 1-hour lunch break. Then 1300 to 1700. Once you started, you could end whenever you finished the exam, but the time allotted was 4 hours per exam session.

License exams are a part of the Kings Point experience. This photo is the class of 2013 sitting in O'Hara Hall in the identical setting that the class of 1971 sat over 40-years earlier.

The exams were highly structured, so we knew what was coming the following day and used the evening before to just bone up for the last time, but made sure to get enough sleep to pace ourselves. After five days, we were entirely drained and out of juice in our batteries. That weekend was non-stop sleep, and we only got up to eat and worry about our final grades. When grades came in the following week, there was a huge celebration. Yes, there were a few that didn't make it, but I could not have been happier to receive my average mid-80s score. It's astonishing that I can still remember that number! In a week, we'd be throwing our hats in the air. We did nothing for a week except prepare for leaving for the last time and making plans for the next events in our lives. While we had been at Kings Point for four years, by the time we graduated we had matured more than eight years. It played well for us as we entered the real world with a sizable leg up over other new college graduates.

At the end of the first week of June, before a packed audience on Tomb Field on a bright, beautiful day, we took our oath as commissioned officers, received our diplomas and threw our hats in the air. Let life after Kings Point begin!

Epilog to Four Years at Kings Point

The inscription on my yearbook reads "These were the best and the worst years of my life. The longest days and the shortest years." I suppose if you ask any graduate, they will concur. There is nothing fun about spending nine months subjected to the rigors of being a plebe at any service academy. No matter our class year, whenever we were restricted to the Academy, especially in the dead of winter, the place was downright desolate. There was almost no one else around and the weekend days seemed to drag on forever while everyone else was away on liberty. Your girlfriend, if you had one, was annoyed with you for doing whatever you did that resulted in your restriction and the ruination of her weekend plans.

Acta Non Verba and More

Most every Kings Point graduate will agree that in many ways they guided their life around the motto we etched in our beings of Acta Non Verba – Deeds, Not Words. Many of us applied this mantra to both our professional and personal lives almost to a fault. Most of us are driven to work hard each day and night without complaint or objection. We may not have spent much time in management training classes, but we unmistakably learned how to be a leader and, thus, extremely good at managing and motivating the people that worked for and with us. We learned how to lead by example, and this was essentially a result of osmosis from our four-year Academy experience. Probably one of the exceptional benefits we learned starting with our plebe training was how to focus. Multitasking is overrated, and those that can focus have the distinct advantage to produce vast amounts of high-quality results.

We left the Academy, frequently in our early twenties - physically. However, mentally and built on our Academy life experience, we were surely in our late twenties. New graduates from "regular" college and people we competed against for positions in our professional lives were far less mature, aware of their environs, and respectful of other people in general. Kings Point provided us with a six to eight-year maturity and experience advantage.

Some of the many things that I learned and applied throughout my life was the ability to get along with people all over the world without conflict and without fear that something might happen to me or I would get into personal danger. I learned during my sea year experience that there are places in every city or town that you just need to steer clear of. I also learned how to avoid being an "Ugly American," a nearly obsolete term that is still meaningful elsewhere in the world. I spent the majority of my career involved in business relationships with non-Americans, and I thank Kings Point for the gift they gave me. I learned through my Academy experience the principle of cause and effect, and I've always been aware of it without obsessing over it. I only needed to dig a little into history, to understand "the story" that impacted situations I was confronting. My professional focus has been in the Asian countries, and since we learned so little about Asia during our secondary education, I was motivated to read and understand the history of the countries where I was actively involved. I've always been far more interested in the events of the past 100 years than the period much beyond that – that's just my personal preference.

I have no doubt whatsoever that the experiences my classmates and I had during our four years were significantly different than classes that graduated 10 years before us and certainly those who graduated 10 years after us. Today cannot be anything like it was nearly 50 years ago! The impact that my four-year experience had on the rest of my life is what caused me to devote the hundreds of hours I've spent writing this chronicle about Kings Point. This story began as a single chapter of a book I've been writing to tell the story of my experiences moving several sectors of manufacturing to Asia and detail the reasons why they will never return to our shores no matter the political circumstances. It was my very close friend and former roommate, Tom, who urged me to put more into this "chapter" than I originally planned. While hundreds of books have been written about the other military academies, I could find only a few about Kings Point and none with a first-hand account of our unique life while attending.

Made in the USA
Lexington, KY
22 November 2017